BECOMING
& BELONGING

BECOMING & BELONGING
BELONGING

A Practical Design for Confirmation

EDITED BY

WILLIAM R. MYERS

CONTRIBUTORS

GARY HALSTEAD

BRENDA KINDER

RICHARD KIRCHHERR

WILLIAM R. MYERS

TIMOTHY NELSON

&

RICHARD WOLF

UNITED CHURCH PRESS
CLEVELAND, OHIO

United Church Press, Cleveland, Ohio 44115
© 1993 by William R. Myers

Biblical quotations
are from the New Revised Standard Version
of the Bible, © 1989 by the Division of Christian Education
of the National Council of the Churches of Christ
in the U.S.A., and are used by permission

Printed in the United States of America
The paper used in this publication is acid-free
and meets the minimum requirements
of American National Standard for Information
Sciences-Permanence of Paper
for Printed Library Materials,
ANSI Z39.48-1984

98 97 96 95 94 93   5 4 3 2 1

Library of Congress Cataloging-in-Publication Data

Becoming and belonging : a practical design for confirmation /
edited by William R. Myers ; contributors, Gary
Halstead . . . [et al.].
p.   cm.
Includes bibliographical references and index.
ISBN 0-8298-0942-2 (alk. paper)
1. Confirmation—United Church of Christ.
2. Christian education of teenagers.
3. Church work with teenagers.
4. United Church of Christ—Membership.
5. Reformed Church—Membership.
6. Congregational churches—Membership.
I. Myers, William, 1942–   .
II. Halstead, Gary.
BX9886.B43   1993
234'.162—dc20
93-23349
CIP

*To those
who continue
to nurture
the faith
of the church's
youth.*

Contents

Acknowledgments   ix

Introduction by Sara Little   xi

Part 1. A Working Theory of Confirmation   1

   1. Confirmation as Rite of Passage   3
   – The Early Church   4
   – Merger of Church and State   5
   – Reformation's Confirmation Setting   6
   – The American Context   8

   2. Becoming and Belonging   11
   – Congregational Identity   12
   – Witnesses to a Covenant   14
   – A Story to Tell: Tradition   15
   – Taking a Spiritual Journey: Pilgrimage   16
   – Together a Faithful Community: Ministry   17
   – Summary: Four Core Conditions   18

   3. Embodying Four Core Conditions   23
   – David and a Confirmation Team   24
   – The Thursday-Sunday Sequence   28
   – Critical Reflection on the Model   31
   – Summary   33

   4. Pastor Jim's Strategy   35
   – The Small Congregation   36
   – The Model in the Pastor's Mind   37
   – A Three-Phase, Multi-Year Confirmation Experience   40
   – Critical Reflection on the Model   41
   – Summary   42

5. A Confirmation Colloquy 45
 – The Models of Confirmation   45
 – Dueling Cultures of Meaning   47
 – Cross-Generational Leadership   51
 – The Politics of Worship   52
 – Telling the Story   54
 – The Presence of the Holy Spirit   57
 – Marginalized Members   59
6. Youth, Spirituality, and the Church 61
 – A Curriculum of Transcendence   61
 – Wading in the Water   62
 – Youth in Church   63
 – Becoming Intentional   64
 – Summary   66

Part 2. Resources for Confirmation 67
 7. We Covenant with the Lord and One with Another 69
   Experience 1: Heirs of the Covenant   71
   Experience 2: Hanging of the Greens   72
   Experience 3: Talking History   73
   Experience 4: Sanctuary Search   75
   Experience 5: World's Greatest Chain Letter   77
   Focus Event on Covenant: Community   79
 8. Experiencing the Tradition 91
   Experience 6: Who Is Jesus?   93
   Experience 7: Chalcedon   95
   Experience 8: Encountering Parables   97
   Experience 9: Singing the Lord's Song   100
   Experience 10: Luther and the Reformation   101
   Focus Event on Tradition: Ten from the Top   102
 9. Pilgrimage 115
   Experience 11: The Water of Life   117
   Experience 12: Holy Ground   120
   Experience 13: Flooded Moments   124

Experience 14: Meditative Prayer   127

Experience 15: The Letter   131

Focus Event on Pilgrimage: Christ's Claim   134

10. Ministry   141

Experience 16: Making Golden Calves   143

Experience 17: "Let My People Go!"   146

Experience 18: CROP Walk   150

Experience 19: The Church with Its Sleeves Rolled Up   152

Experience 20: A Children's Ward   154

Focus Event on Ministry: A Footwashing Experience   155

**11. A Partial Review of the Literature:
Confirmation Curricula in Theory and Practice**   159

Appendixes

A. New Member's Covenant   177

B. The Letter   179

Notes   185

Selected Bibliography   189

Index   193

Acknowledgments

Thank you to the Lilly Endowment and its support for the Union Theological Seminary of Richmond, Virginia's "Youth Ministry and Theological Schools" project, of which this study was one small component; our consistently excellent typists, Ms. Carol Lach of First Congregational Church, LaGrange, Illinois, and Ms. Linda Parrish of Chicago Theological Seminary; the youth confirmands who experienced the authors' leadership in the sixty or more separate confirmation programs led by the authors as well as in the Chicago Theological Seminary's hosting of two regional confirmation leadership workshops and two confirmation days.

Introduction

Confirmation is one of today's "live" topics in conversations and conferences related to the church's educational ministry in general or to youth ministry in particular. Within the last month, I have read or reviewed ten different books, essays, or papers relating to confirmation, almost all of them lamenting the sad state of the confirmation experience. Not one of them gives the kind of help or stirs in me the kind of vision and excitement I feel as I read *Becoming and Belonging*. If I could recommend only one book on confirmation, this would be it.

One reason I am so pleased with the book, of course, is that it is a concrete outcome of the Lilly Endowment funded project, "Youth Ministry and Theological Schools," which I directed for Union Theological Seminary in Richmond, Virginia. Seeking to relate theological school studies to the active practice of youth ministry, the project involved seminary professors with a variety of pastors, educators, seminarians, and congregations. William R. ("Bill") Myers was a member of the Chicago Seminar, a group of professors who met regularly for four years to consider issues and research in youth ministry and to reflect on a series of investigations carried out by members in their own settings. Bill received a grant from the project to call a conference, then to follow through with the working group who produced this book on confirmation. The five pastors (who together have led some sixty confirmation groups) who worked with Bill wrote out of their experience; they know the concerns we face daily as we plan for our ministry with young people.

There are some other reasons I like the book. The introductory chapters provide one of the most interesting, readable, and helpful theological and historical approaches to confirmation that I have read; it places our decisions in solid background context. More than that, it does what too many approaches to confirmation do not do—it relates that background to the contemporary situation and to the suggestions it offers. Those practical ideas are not just clever tricks to involve people. They become a window into the faithfulness of congregations. Young people experience the invitation of transcendence. The interconnectedness of theory and practice, of theology and life, speaks to one of my most cherished principles about how we should "do" Christian education. This book came into being by relating theory and practice, a fact that is clearly communicated.

Consider the title, *Becoming and Belonging*—an inspired title, I call it! It captures the essence of confirmation in a way that expresses what is needed in our time. Confirmation (or confirmation/commissioning) is rooted in the faith of the congregation. It is more than a "program." Although I think there are more "good" and worthwhile approaches than are recognized in the introductory chapters of the book, I do think the need for rethinking and redoing confirmation is urgent. And the careful rethinking, combined with ideas for different approaches, twenty different "experiences," and four different "focus events," as proposed in this book, become a major resource that will surely influence our future work in confirmation.

The fact that the book was produced as a team effort says something about how to carry on confirmation in our time. Pastors will find themselves not *excluded*, but offered a stimulus for a new and vital approach to confirmation. The beneficiaries will be not only young people, but also the congregation as it carries out the four "core conditions" of covenant, tradition, pilgrimage, and ministry around which the whole approach is organized. I commend it to those who care about young people and about the future of the church.

Sara Little

PART ONE

A Working Theory of Confirmation

CHAPTER ONE

Confirmation as Rite of Passage

For Christians... Biological, social, cultural or religious
passages are *rehearsals* or *encores* of the passover in Christ.
Dying and rising with Christ gives a home, a meaning
and a direction to all other human passages.

James Wilde[1]
Confirmed as Children, Affirmed as Teens

Sitting in the confirmation workshop are twenty-six ordained ministers who remind one another that their churches equate religious education with schooling. This means, they say, that confirmation is expected to be a class laden with a substantial curriculum that they, as ordained pastors, must teach. Most of them believe that the class/school/instructional format is expected, even if they are not particularly enthusiastic about this situation. While the times and format for confirmation might vary, all the pastors agree that confirmation is understood by most parents as "the last chance of the church" to impact their children.

Asked to reflect on their own confirmation experiences, one pastor responds that his "recollection of confirmation is very sketchy," but he remembers "confirmation was very much related to the experience of early high school." Like public school, confirmation for him "was compulsory." It was clear: "You went to this class at the church because this is what you did in ninth grade." He continues:

I have a yellowed newspaper photograph of myself and several other confirmands involved in some activity related to the confirmation program. Although like myself, two others in the picture later became ordained clergy, I cannot remember being present for that photo. I think the class took place on Saturday mornings. A minister was in

3

charge, and we memorized a creed but I don't remember what it was.
We memorized some scripture, but I don't remember what it was.[1]

Conversation turns to the fact that, whatever the terms used to describe confirmation, the mainline denominations represented by this workshop are shrinking, while research in this area partially attributes such membership decline to a confirmation pattern that seems to graduate youth out of the church.[2] One Presbyterian (U.S.A.) pastor responds that this isn't news to him:

> For years I've been aware of the church's confirmation "square dance." By this I mean that when, in the reception of new members, we "extend the right hand of fellowship" in worship to those members of the confirmation class we then "alleman left" them out the front door and into the church's "inactive" file. . . . What we have in the rite of confirmation is a graduation ceremony out of the church's school. Their parents have told them that if they do this [graduate from confirmation and join the church] then they can make up their own minds about whether or not to attend church. Most don't.[3]

The Early Church

Such a description of confirmation would have made no sense to a Christian from the early church. At that time, a few centuries after Christ, confirmation was part of an initiation sequence (baptism/confirmation/eucharist) marking the believer's commencement of a radically different life. Consisting of an anointing (following baptism), a sealing with the sign of the cross, and the laying on of hands, confirmation anticipated a new believer's involvement in ministry as symbolized by the broken bread and spilled wine of the communion table.[4] *Metanoia*, a "change of heart" essential and central to this initiation sequence, suggested that new converts were to be spirit-filled and powerfully different from those persons who continued to live their lives based on the expectations of the dominant culture within which they were immersed.

Recognizing the degree of tension existing between the Christian and the then-dominant Roman culture, "the early church saw the convert's first burst of enthusiasm for what it was: a fragile reality that was apt to evaporate as quickly as it appeared."[5] Because of this awareness, intentional structures like those of the Alexandria Catechetical School attempted to nurture and challenge new converts through a careful instructional sacramental process.[6] Other institutions, including local congregations, emphasized a similar "immersion" within the teachings and practices of the faithful. In other words, to *become* Christian in the early days of the church was to *belong* to an experiential way of life radically different from the practices of the dominant culture.

Merger of Church and State

Constantine's conversion (313 C.E.) mandated Christianity as the state-approved religion and within the next hundred years sharply altered the way confirmation occurred. Unfortunately, persons who became Christian in order to be approved and to earn a living within this new political context often would go through the required motions without necessarily experiencing a radical change of heart (*metanoia*). Thus, where "being Christian" once had meant having to complete something along the lines of a three-year immersion within the catechumenate, the state now accepted as politically employable (as Christian) those who had enrolled but had not yet completed the process. Once the hurdle of achieving Christian status (and a resultant job) was behind them, these adult "converts" often went about business as usual. Meanwhile, the church, swollen by sheer numbers, continued to adjust expectations downward. Becoming Christian unfortunately was equated with becoming employable as a Roman citizen.

Those who attended catechetical classes often were bored; note one pastor's rebuke from no less than Saint Augustine, Bishop of Hippo: "You have had, moreover, to acknowledge and complain that often, because you talked too long and with too little enthusiasm, it has befallen you to become commonplace and wearisome even to yourself, not to mention him whom you were trying to instruct by your discourse, and others who were present."[7] Given such circumstances, by the conclusion of the sixth century confirmation and infant baptism, the logical conclusions of a now politically dominant and established church, were separated into two rites. Babies were baptized by local pastors and grew within an established church; when "of age," they were "confirmed" as full members by the traveling bishop. Initially an integral part of the adult conversion/initiation process of baptism, confirmation, through such historical alterations, began to play a new role as the "member-intake" system for the children of the state-approved church. By this process the children of adult believers were enfranchised and entitled to the bounty of the state and the promise of the church.

Reformation's Confirmation Setting

Even the Reformation could not redress this historical trend. It has been said, for example, that John Calvin's theocracy, his wedding of church and state in Geneva, assumed that the entire society (the state) provided the appropriate context of the church's confirmation:

> John Knox described it [Calvin's Geneva] as "a school of Jesus Christ," with "edification" the purpose of Calvinist worship. Calvin was a theologian who waged a lifelong battle against what he considered theological ignorance, and so the didactic element of all worship was high. At the same time the Calvinist system of Geneva subjected the populace to a discipline so rigid and so thoroughly enforced as to make the harshest novice masters grow pale.[8]

In those countries with state churches, confirmation became the means for determining the right to vote, setting tax lists, and keeping population records. This merger of the church with the needs of the state ensured political allegiance by those confirmed to particular "home" churches. Writing on the entangling importance of confirmation, Richard Baxter noted that confirmation could never be described as a "mere" catechizing into the historic faith of the church: "We take it [confirmation] to be the approbation of the personal profession of *them that claim a title to the church-state*, and *privilege of the adult*, and an investing them solemnly therein, upon the solemn renewal (and personal adult entrance) into covenant with God."[9]

While confirmation came to be identified with a set of classes for children, its completion marked the end of a child's formal schooling, initiated the possibility of marriage, the opportunity to leave the parish, and the ability "to work, join a guild, attend a state school, or go off to boarding school."[10] Confirmation thus pragmatically came to serve as the doorway (an authentic rite of passage) into the privileges and responsibilities of adulthood as a full citizen within the broader culture. By the eighteenth century,

> In a number of places in Europe, a young person of fourteen could join the work force and be treated as a citizen. Some congregations included the duties of citizenship in their catechetical programs. They even had courses on health to help those who were about to be married. It was not at all odd to have young ladies postponing their confirmation a year or two so that they could use the occasion as a kind of coming-out party to announce to the public that they were available for marriage.[11]

Because confirmation had become the cultural rite opening the way into adulthood/citizenship/church membership, it also became the celebration of the "great festival of youth." The confirmation sermon was a high point of this "great festival." One ran fifty-three pages long; another ran twenty-eight pages following the examination.[12] Along with lengthy sermons, the public confirmation examinations were extended. In addition, a confession of faith, usually written by the confirmands, was expected, and a vow or oath, was taken:

> Some of the theatrical extravagances may be seen in one [pastor's] addresses. He told his confirmands: "You have sworn! God has heard it! He will judge you not only in the far-off eternity but now already, here already. . . . Oh, hold fast, hold fast to what you have vowed for your welfare in time and eternity.[13]

Consecrating each confirmand with a special Bible passage for memorization, the pastor sent youth from the chancel into the congregation so that they might beg their parents' forgiveness and seek their blessing.[14] In addition,

> Many other external customs became associated with the day to make it more significant: antiphonal songs between the children and the

congregation or between the confirmands and the school children, flo-
ral wreaths and foliage decorating the church, dramatic ringing of the
bells at the proper moment, and special clothes for the event. Like
baptism and marriages, confirmation became an occasion for great
family festivity.[15]

Considering such practices of "religious education" (understanding this in the broadest and deepest sense), Sören Kierkegaard
noted that this "thing of becoming and of being a Christian is now
a triviality."[16] He expanded his concern with this comment: "Confirmation then is easily seen to be far deeper nonsense than infant
baptism, precisely because confirmation claims to supply what
was lacking in infant baptism: a real personality which can con-
sciously assume responsibility for a vow which has to do with the
decision of an external blessedness."[17]

While many proposals for reform appeared in the following
decades, confirmation as the approved church/state entry into
membership/citizenship (truly a cultural rite of passage) had
become so deeply rooted in the religious, social, educational, political, and cultural life of the people that no one dared attack it.
Confirmation would denote the end of childhood; it would assume
importance as the cultural/religious doorway into adulthood; it
would mark those confirmed as church members; it would also be
the portal to full political citizenship.

The American Context

From the earliest days of the American republic, the assumption by churches that white, Anglo-Saxon Protestants formed the
backbone of the nation clarified the role of confirmation. Protestant
denominations drew the designation "mainline," and while the
American church-state context was not the same as the European
setting, being a member of a mainline congregation automatically
connected youth within the dominant culture and enabled confirmation to function as a rite of passage into American adulthood in
much the same way it had in Europe.

But, as mainline denominations grew less certain of their

dominant cultural status, the social invention of adolescence in the late nineteenth century worked to downplay confirmation as the preferred rite of passage into adulthood.[18] With adolescence came a postponement of cultural adulthood. In addition, while throughout the nineteenth century confirmation had remained the major marker into church/state adulthood, churches began to discover in the twentieth-century context that American youth became adults through a myriad of individualistic ways other than confirmation—they dropped out of school, got a job, owned a car, bore children, joined the military, completed high school, got married, or graduated from college or trade school. Any one of these activities began to be more clearly associated with cultural adulthood than the once-dominant practice of confirmation. Given the church's weakened role as cultural gatekeeper in the modern era, confirmation as rite of passage into cultural adulthood soon became a hollow exercise.

The current question facing the church as it once again considers what role, if any, confirmation plays, is, what is Christianity in this modern context, or indeed, who is Christ for us today? If the answer is, in part, that the church is called to be a vibrant faith community incarnating Christ's presence and welcoming adolescents into age-appropriate shared ministry, then we cannot simply *think* through to such an answer. Confirmation as a hollow graduation exercise from a school is not enough. Neither is the now-empty assertion that confirmation should be a cultural and religious rite of passage. An answer to the issue of confirmation, so compellingly different from the reality experienced by the majority of adolescents attending mainline churches today must be lived into, emerging as the outcome of daring Christian practice. We use the adjective "daring" because being a vibrant welcoming faith community suggests *becoming* something more like the early church while remaining fully aware of the contemporary context, that is, *belonging* to an incarnation of a fundamentally different way of seeing life, of thinking about it, and of living it within the current pluralistic culture. It is to this challenge that we now turn.

CHAPTER TWO

Becoming and Belonging

We already have too many people who know something
about Jesus, *about* the church. What we need is people who
will follow Jesus, who will be the church.

Stanley Hauerwas and
William H. Willimon
Resident Aliens

Becoming and *belonging* are relational words that necessarily intersect within the contemporary invention of adolescence; that is, that
which the adolescent "I" is *becoming* is met by persons, ideas,
tasks, and institutions to which "I" hope to "pledge my troth" and
come to *belong*. In an earlier time, becoming and belonging occurred as adults and those we now call adolescents worked side by
side in the field, home, and other cultural institutions, including
the church. In our busy, modern, complex existence, however, the
absence of mentoring adults, appropriate and helpful job experiences, as well as welcoming communities within which intergenerational interaction is the norm have made the assigned task
of adolescence—the achievement of personal identity within society—extremely difficult. Not that millions of adolescents don't
achieve identity and come to function within society, because it is
obvious that such occurs; but, from the church's point of view, a
satisfactory "becoming" is not so obvious. Christians, presumably,
are not the same as citizens. Being a Christian may be the same as
being a citizen, but the once-assumed religious connection as well
as the cultural advantage held by citizens who are Christians is no
longer a certainty. To be Christian in late twentieth-century America may be to assume a position without privilege, an unrecogniz-
able situation only a few decades ago. We need, therefore, to ask

11

what a community self-identified as Christian really is, and if within such a community there is a particular perspective or message worth sharing and passing on to future generations. Perhaps a negative answer to this question—that the institutional Protestant church with its canned confirmation program and its resultant graduation exercise—are of no worth—means that the church has outlived its usefulness. If this is true, confirmation as a practice of the church has no point at all, and churches might better spend limited time and resources elsewhere.

Congregational Identity

However, if a local congregation may recognize that its current disenfranchised status actually mirrors the early church's experience of being something other than what was honored within that pre-Constantinian Roman (not Christian) dominant culture. Perhaps such a congregation will come to understand, out of its own peculiar calling as a Christian community, that confirmation has a distinctive purpose and is an age-appropriate rite of the church for children raised within its unique community of faith. For a congregation that can recognize itself in this picture, confirmation is needed as much for the adults as for the youth as it can become a focal point for clarifying congregational identity. And, when adolescents from such a community of faith are challenged by the outside world, the church so identified (as having a hope-filled story) can open its doors to them in as many ways as possible, welcoming them through a variety of rites, including confirmation, into that caring community. In such a church one might hope that living, authentic witnesses of all ages will interact with each other and with God in a shared, common ministry. Through such a process, a faithful church can make its proclamation, claim a common baptism into ministry, and provide a way by which an older generation appropriately witnesses to the becoming and belonging of the younger generations.

In order to make such an affirmation, we must recognize that confirmation in the eyes of contemporary society is not a real rite of passage. In addition, Western society has invented adolescence and designated it as a time when youth are not expected to be of much value, when they are not yet persons. They are also expected, out of an individualistic ethos, to make their own way into adulthood without much help from the dominant culture. The church's claim that they are (already) persons of worth may come as a surprise to adolescents and others. Nevertheless, the church that recognizes the tension existing between the expectations of our culture and the covenantal significance of baptism can begin to understand confirmation as a rite that confirms a personal acceptance by the confirmand of baptismal vows, carrying an accompanying increase in the ministerial responsibilities of new community members, and affirming—in real ways—the vocation of both its adolescent and adult believers. Viewed in this four-fold fashion, the covenantal faithfulness of a church is suspect to the degree that it fails to accept and integrate into the congregation those adolescents and adults who complete such a faithful process.

Because the rite of confirmation, in this sense, is a window into the faithfulness of congregational practice, it should be recognized, emphasized, intentionally pursued, and celebrated. This perspective affords both congregation and confirmand a rare occasion for joint growth and celebration. But this can occur only if congregations support, in the presence of older youth and adults as "living bridges"—witnesses, storytellers, spiritual guides, companions, and co-ministers—a variety of healthy, purposeful roles for adults and confirmands within the ongoing practices of the church. The faith stance that identifies the church (God knows, loves, and affirms the worth of all peoples, including adolescents) must be incarnated, or practiced, in real ways. Given this position, it would seem natural that these congregations develop confirmation teams composed of adults and youth, claiming such as layministry, as well as regularly involving youth in the centering practices of the congregation. Among these practices should be the preparation and leadership of common worship, including the sermon. In addition, involvement in ministry, mission, and service, as regular practices of the congregation, should challenge both youth and adults not only toward vocational faithfulness, but also into a recognition of their own spiritual pilgrimages.

Given such a vision, while certain models of confirmation have risen and fallen throughout the history of confirmation, the following four core conditions can be said to undergird all good contemporary models of confirmation and are understood by the authors of this book to be potentially suggestive for such a full-bodied incarnation of confirmation: (1) covenant, (2) tradition, (3) pilgrimage, and (4) the shared ministry of the congregation.

Witnesses to a Covenant

Covenant, the first core condition for confirmation, strongly borrows from the English sixteenth-century Puritan movement. Believing that while everyone was baptized within the state church, few were serious about faith or holiness, the Puritans expected confirmation to be a rite in which the believer pledged fidelity to Christ and congregation. Toward this end, local identification of church covenants was emphasized, with Puritans baptizing their children in specific parishes.

> *So a literature developed reflecting a style of self-examination, which emphasized the awakening from carelessness about one's condition, the recognition of the grip of sin, the readiness for the stirrings of the divine life within. When the signs of the work of God were clear, an unbeliever could be brought into the church, or a child could "own the covenant."*[1]

In contemporary churches, the first core condition would accent the close connection of the congregation with the confirmand and would serve as a guide toward building a meaningful understanding of covenant into the confirmation process. This process would therefore actively engage faithful witnesses or ritual elders in the life of the confirmands, working shoulder to shoulder, a confirmation ministry team sharing their own understanding of faith and owning the covenant through service, worship, prayer, and the experience of practicing covenantal community with confirmands. Older adolescent church members would be expected to engage in their own practice of ministry by becoming team members. Chapter 6 offers five practical covenantal experiences and a focus event centered around the idea of mentoring adolescents.

A Story to Tell: Tradition

A second core condition, *tradition*, has to do with how confirmands come to understand those faithful persons who have gone before and how churches might better go about the intentional retelling of the story of their tradition. We approach tradition, however, not as a dead topic, but as a journey (a traditioning process) that confirmands are invited to enter and claim as "their" story. In this sense, tradition is an ongoing dialogue composed of many voices. Discovering "our" story in conjunction with the traditioning process is a multilayered event. People therefore "hear" the story in ways other than the merely cognitive. While we read, for example, that Luther assumed confirmation to be a churchly rite offering an excellent opportunity for content-based catechetical instruction, his lively teaching style relied upon a dynamic question/answer process utilizing penny-posters as a visual shorthand that presented openings for those who had gathered with him to discuss the essence of faith. Luther would introduce a poster; the confirmands would join him in discussion. When published in book form, these penny-posters unfortunately were set down in what appeared to be a final form and were named *The Small Catechism*:

> *Contrary to the way* The Small Catechism *is often used today (like a computer mechanically punching out sterile bits of information), Luther wanted it used as an opportunity for dialogue, exploring the meanings and the ramifications of Christian teachings for each person in his own situation. Further, Luther planned his catechisms for use by the whole Christian community; not only children, but older youth and adults. You have only to read his letters counseling those who sought his help or eavesdrop at the discussions he had with his friends around the dinner table to see how he practiced what he preached. In addition, some years he preached as many as four different series of sermons on the elements of the catechism. Personally, he noted, part of his daily devotions was to meditate on portions of the catechism.*[2]

Unfortunately, those who followed Luther turned his simple catechetical style into ever longer, more abstract, and more elaborate theological treatises. By so doing, they squeezed the lively process of a confirmand's faith pilgrimage with tradition into a rote response to a catechism. Luther's multilevel, often sensual embodiment of the Christian story got lost.

In the contemporary congregation, telling the story of faith must recapture Luther's lively, personal, relational, interactive style of teaching. As the dry lecture, complete with exams, accepts as normative only one learning style, mimics our culturally dominant schooling model, and avoids incarnational contact of the sort usually present in Luther's discussion, we attempt in chapter 7 to offer experiential ways that storytellers, dramatists, artists, or teachers ("rabbis") might immerse the confirmand relationally within the faith-story.

Taking a Spiritual Journey: Pilgrimage

A third core condition, *pilgrimage*, refers to the individual's spiritual journey, a concept perhaps most ascendant in the historical movement of Pietism. Working in Lutheran church contexts in which nearly everyone had been baptized, the Pietists were led by Philip Spener (1635–1705) in a criticism of the increasingly heavy, formal, and intellectual Lutheran orthodoxy. Affirming a subjective, inward acceptance of Christ as Lord (a concern of the heart as well as the head), Pietists hoped that processes like confirmation would create groups of true believers. Thus, their intense confirmation process emphasized a subjective belief stance rather than an objective knowledge of the faith. Emphasizing the confirmation ceremony as (1) a solemn vow-taking, (2) a witness to one's personal faith, and (3) a commitment to the obligations of a Christian way of life, Pietists pushed confirmands to surrender publicly to Christ, recite personal scripture readings, and be welcomed into the body of Christ, or the church. For the Pietists, confirmation and the related sacrament of first communion initiated church membership.

In considering the best of this historic movement, we believe that contemporary congregations must become involved with the contemporary experience and the spiritual journey of each confirmand, undergirding and accompanying that journey with spiritual guides, companions, directors, and guarantors, that is, older believers in the faith. Chapter 8 carries five experiences centering and naming this process, as well as a focus event.

Together a Faithful Community: Ministry

The fourth core condition, *ministry*, involves the practice of service that occurs when a person is engaged as an active participant (or baptized minister) in the faithful body of Christ, the church. This is the part of every baptized minister's vocational calling. The early church understood that while everyone baptized was called (*vocatio*) into ministry, this vocation of ministry was not reserved for the professional; instead, *everyone* was a minister. The Protestant tradition, claiming a priesthood of all believers, understood that ministry could and should be a part of every vocation. In the contemporary church, however, it often appears to the observer that ministry and call are the sole property of the ordained clergy.

Perhaps the deep history of the church regarding the ministerial role of every baptized member comes to the surface through the often routinized activities of the American mainline confirmation work camp experience. In the best of such work camps, confirmands report their often exuberant discovery of what really counts in life. For example, consider the words of a work camper as reported in Tom Montgomery-Fate's excellent photo-essay on work camps, *Building Worlds/Challenging Boundaries:*

> My nails are ragged, my fingers and cuticles sore, and I have tar still sticking to my skin. But even so, the physical changes that occurred to my body and even to the house we worked on are largely superficial. The greater changes that can and must occur are not purely material. We need to keep our spiritual vision alive to activate our hands.[3]

These comments appear to reflect the church's deep tradition regarding ministry (expected of every baptized member) and vocation (a clarion call to serve, each according to their gifts).

All too frequently, however, the work camp (and the accompanying sense of ministry/vocation) is a one-time excursion outside the normal ongoing activities and programs of the local congregation. Only when a variety of ministries are practiced and accessible for all members regardless of age can we assume that the words "welcome to the *ministry* of Jesus Christ" will have meaning for the confirmand. Lila Watson, an Appalachian native and someone to whom the work campers in Montgomery-Fate's book had come to minister, put it like this: "If you have come to help me, you are wasting your time. But if you have come because your liberation is bound up with mine, then let us work together."[4]

In another context, the editor of this book has stated,

> *I have come to believe that our culture treats adolescents like small children while intentionally isolating them from meaningful work. This is also unfortunately true of the American "mainline" congregations—we ask youth what they intend to be when they "grow up," yet we fail to connect them with spirit-filled mentors who might appropriately introduce them to possible vocations.*[5]

Leaders in the confirmation process who understand these central categories of ministry and vocation will undertake to include the confirmand within a variety of churchly practices, encouraging the confirmand to experience the possibilities of vocational ministry. Chapter 9 suggest five experiences to emphasize the integral role such an understanding of ministry can play in confirmation. That chapter concludes with a summary on "footwashing" as one potential congregational/confirmation/ministry vehicle.

Summary: Four Core Conditions

Table 1 summarizes the four core conditions of covenant, tradition, pilgrimage, and congregation. All function simultaneously within the life of the church and the confirmand.

Core conditions such as these provide one way congregations can evaluate their current practices regarding confirmation. If a congregation agrees with the assumptions undergirding each condition, then the conditions can serve as a helpful screen for asking

TABLE 1
Four Core Conditions for Confirmation

The historic emphasis	in which confirmation intentionally is	and leaders serve as
COVENANT	a mentoring process initiating youth into a faithful community	members of a confirmation team, faithful witnesses, or ritual elders.
TRADITION	an experiential immersion within the faith-story of the faithful community	storytellers, dramatists, artists, or teachers ("rabbis").
PILGRIMAGE	the spiritual journey of the faithful individual and the faithful community	spiritual guides, directors, or guarantors.
MINISTRY	a lifelong engagement (vocation) as one of the faithful members of the body of Christ in the practices of that body	co-celebrants, co-pastors, or co-ministers.

questions of the congregation and modifying current confirmation practices. For example, if a congregation affirms these four core conditions and nevertheless continues to charge the minister with the sole responsibility of teaching a set confirmation curriculum over a nine-month period in a classroom setting, then a critical assessment of "what is going on in confirmation" might uncover the following questions and possible modifications. (See Table 2.)

After such an evaluation, a creative ministry team, commissioned into service might design a confirmation process that would look quite different from what had previously occurred. What follows, in chapter 3, is a look inside such a model as seen by

TABLE 2
Applying the Core Conditions to the Confirmation Process

The Core Condition	Posing the Question about Current Practice	Possible Modification to the Confirmation Process
COVENANT	*Q:* Are witnesses of varying ages actively involved in sharing their faith with these "heirs of the covenant"? *A:* No, the pastor is the only older person who meets with the youth.	The congregation could commission slightly older youth and adults of varying ages as a confirmation team to actively mentor these confirmands.
TRADITION	*Q:* Is the story and tradition of the faith told in ways that connect with the life-experience of the confirmands? *A:* No, the pastor presents a series of lectures, and discussion is limited.	The confirmation team could actively engage the confirmands through a variety of experiential learning strategies focusing on the faith story of the church.
PILGRIMAGE	*Q:* Does this church adequately address, engage, nurture, and challenge the spiritual journey of the confirmands? *A:* At this time no spiritual language	A reflection process could take seriously personal faith and the history and story of each confirmand and the group as a whole. A retreat on the "language of faith" could initiate this

	seems possible. Prayer is not a part of the class, and no clear connection of the spiritual journey within the confirmand's life is attempted.	process. The discipline of prayer would be central to such a retreat.
MINISTRY	*Q:* Are confirmands regularly involved in the ongoing life and practice of the congregation? *A:* No, the class meets in a parallel fashion with the church. No confirmand is active in any church role. Age-graded activities have occurred since birth.	Confirmands could gradually become more involved in the worship, mission, and ministering life of the congregation. Involvement in worship could initiate this process. Committee membership and an active role in some central activities of the church could follow.

a high school student named David who serves in such a program. Chapter 4 considers the same program through the eyes of Pastor Jim, the person who moved from the class-based, lecture style to the staff-designed, experiential model.

CHAPTER THREE

Embodying Four Core Conditions

The language of religion is the vehicle of collective
experience and it is meaningful only when it speaks of
experience and addresses itself to experience.

Dorothee Soelle
Death by Bread Alone

Confirmation has taken a variety of formats within the American church context. There are models, for example, that last two years, one month, eight weeks, or four Saturdays, that get framed, for example, as a class meeting every Sunday for two years, as three retreats, or as a summer camp. The norm, however, seems to be the nine-month format of the academic year (the confirmation class) held once per week solely with the pastor as teacher. Whatever shape a congregation's confirmation program takes, however, if that congregation sees confirmation as both a rite and a process incorporating people within the practices of the faith community, rather than as a graduation ceremony, then a reconnection with the four historic movements outlined in chapter 2 will result in radically different confirmation practice. The form may continue, for example, to be a two-year, weekly class, but that form will connect with the community, moving in concert with its practice. No longer will the pastor whose congregation has critically reflected upon these movements labor in isolation apart from them. Instead, a cross-age team of mentoring witnesses will immerse the confirmands within the story, vision, and vocational practices of the members of the Christian faith. Such an immersion, however, assumes an ongoing, intentional, participatory interconnection within the larger faith community. Confirmands are therefore encouraged to engage in acts of ministry even as they play active roles within the faithful practices of the gathered and scattered congregation.

In a small church, the pastor frequently identifies the two to three older adults (including the pastor) and three older youth who might be willing to serve on a confirmation team. One congregation made their initial selection by holding a discussion in which members determined to form their confirmation team around persons whom they felt embodied certain valued qualities. However this choice of a team occurs, it needs to take place three to six months before the confirmands come together for their initial meeting.

David and a Confirmation Team

On the following pages, a high school senior named David (all names are changed) who serves on such a cross-generational team shares what that team does. David summarizes, in his own words, some of the concerns and intentions of his church's confirmation team, which also includes Lynn, a high school junior, Pastor Jim, and Sally, who acted as a confirmation adult advisor. Like many congregations, theirs understands itself to be a small church, currently at one hundred members. This church offers confirmation on a regular basis every third year.

Pastor Jim, Lynn, Sally, and David were charged with their task in the spring, met several times over the summer, and personally contacted the twelve ninth, tenth, and eleventh graders they hoped might wish to be confirmed. Pastor Jim explains how this occurred:

> *With the church council's approval, I asked Sally, an adult layperson, and two high school youth, David and Lynn, to form a "confirmation team" for a year. We took one summer day and spent it in a local park. While swimming, tossing frisbees, and eating hot dogs, we told our own stories and talked about how we could understand what we were to do as a "ministry." We recognized that this would be hard, exciting work, and we set aside a weekend later that summer to tackle some of the details. On that weekend we split into two groups and reworked eight rough session designs I had chosen. We kicked*

those sketches inside out until we owned what was going to take place in each particular session; we then came together and jointly reflected on each other's new designs. We did the same thing with a retreat design I had borrowed from a retreat manual. By the end of this working weekend (one night and one day) we had worked through eight sessions and our initial confirmation retreat; we were exhausted, but we also felt like this was something of importance for our own lives, as well as for the lives of the confirmands.

The enthusiasm from this initial retreat fueled the confirmation team's planning. They continued to pursue those students eligible for confirmation with an invitation for the fall.

Eight youth responded to that invitation, and an early fall weekend retreat was held to initiate the confirmation journey. Thursdays were reserved for team meetings, and confirmation participants gathered at the church every Sunday morning for breakfast and a discussion period. Following breakfast, the entire group would go to Sunday morning worship. David (a senior) relates that an intentional part of the confirmation strategy was slowly to involve the confirmands in the practice of worship:

Because I started out ushering and occasionally reading scripture, I wasn't blown away when Pastor Jim had my confirmation group involved in writing and giving a dialogue sermon. Because I did that, I wasn't terrified when he asked me to preach once last summer. I think it's important that kids—over time—get to be involved in worship.

David also was aware that adolescents are expected to be involved in various ways in this small church: "You know, not everyone wants to do everything, but at least five high school seniors are still strongly connected to this church. One of them even went to Central America to do vaccinations. We had several nurses and doctors from this area that were on the same trip." Pastor Jim adds:

This didn't just happen overnight. We started down this path when we recognized that none of our youth were voluntarily involved at any level of the church, unless they were plugged in by family. We weren't, as a church, very hospitable to youth. For example, no youth had ever read scripture in what was then known as "adult" worship! So six years ago we started this confirmation team idea. We linked the confirmation "curriculum" to worship. We invited youth into the church's ministry. And while some would say it's messy and not neat and clean like some of the canned curriculum we've considered, we're pleased with the results; youth are "in" this church.

Sally offers this reflection:

You have to like people to be on a staff like this one. I'd say that some persons would find it safer to lecture and need more controls than what we have. But we're an enthusiastic bunch, most of the time, and we care about each other. I've done this two years, and it's been a place where I've gotten as much as I've given.

Sally is returning to college next year. She states: "I'll miss this, but I'll see these kids in church."

As the confirmation team, Sally, Pastor Jim, David, and Lynn developed a way of working together that embodies a shared vision. Reflecting on how this occurred, Pastor Jim notes that the confirmation team made a conscious decision to meet every week:

If this team idea was to work, we needed a regular meeting. We had a hunch that a lot of work was involved. We wanted this new way of doing confirmation to happen in a positive way. So we met. I'd often pick up people at school. Usually we'd meet in church or at someone's home. I quickly discovered that as a minister I pastored both the team and the confirmands. I can't overemphasize this. And since the team was modeling ways people could get involved in the church, we began to share leadership responsibilities with the confirmands. Such modeling went beyond the gimmicks of youth ministry "exercises"; it was real. Gradually we got the confirmands into the church's worship process. When this occurred, they began to step outside their role as students and into participatory ministry. What I had hoped might occur, did!

On occasion, the confirmation team had their touchy issues. Lynn had to ask for a leave of absence when her athletic schedule threatened to overwhelm her, and Pastor Jim had to miss several Thursday team meetings because of emergencies. But, as Lynn explains: "So this is life. We knew we'd have to pull together. That's what the word *team* means." "Team" also meant writing community and individual covenants. Jim, David Sally, and Lynn penned these words as "The Confirmation Ministry Team's Covenant":

> We will:
> (1) attend and work at staff meetings;
> (2) be prepared with what we agreed to do;
> (3) get to know each other and the confirmands better;
> (4) continue to find connections in our planning and in our personal lives through the gospel;
> (5) and enjoy the intensity and involvement of what takes place in this ministry.
>
> Sally, David, Lynn, Jim

The Team also decided to write personal covenants; Lynn's began in this fashion:

> *I promise that I will try to concentrate my attention on our planning, to put as much input and thought into the sessions I'm working with as possible. I'll try not to get caught up and let the sometimes melodrama of my life overpower this ministry with the church. I intend to let the people I work with be aware of how I think/feel about God. And I want to grow in my knowledge about God and in how to become more compassionate. Caring is very important to me.*
>
> *Lynn*

Such a confirmation team model as this one has a variety of resources available to it from peer ministry literature.[1] "Peer" is defined not in terms of just one-age cohort, but as persons "who, for the moment at least, are operating at similar levels of behavioral complexity."[2] Such a confirmation ministry with youth and adults therefore begins with the recognition that those who confirm their baptism vows and join a community of faith are welcomed into ministry with Jesus Christ and are to be perceived as co-ministers, members of a priesthood of all believers. Sturdily anchored in responsible church membership, the "everyone a minister" aspect can, within the framework of the presented confirmation ministry model, enable youth to minister with younger peers, functioning as members who *serve* their risen Lord (the early church called this *diakonia*), *proclaim* a special message (called *kerygma*), and are part of a faith-filled *community* (called *koinonia*).

David demonstrates this concept in the journal he kept of the confirmation team's activities. David's journal takes us into a sequence covering a Thursday team meeting, the Sunday morning confirmation meeting, the following Thursday team meeting, and a second Sunday morning confirmation gathering.

The Thursday-Sunday Sequence

Thursday team meeting. Looking ahead, Pastor Jim informed us that he had ordered for the next session the old World's Fair film *Parable*.[3] Lynn, who had seen the film on a church cluster-sponsored program, presented the film's story line and her suggestion that we might use a real live clown. Team discussion centered upon the use of white greasepaint in the film as a symbol of discipleship and resurrection hope. Gradually an idea emerged with Lynn as the clown who, at the end of our time together, would share with each one of us a dab of white greasepaint. This "marking" could be interpreted as an act of inclusion, bringing us together in a unique way. Sally suggested that if we did this, Lynn in clown face might not talk until the very end of the Sunday morning program. Then, as she marked each person, she could share a spoken blessing, a kind of prayer of benediction for them. I had listened to this exchange with growing excitement and added only one further thought, that it sounded as if after we viewed the film someone needed to encourage us to trace through the film's storyline on newsprint or a blackboard so that we could better understand a lot of the symbols in the film. While more work needed to be done, everyone also needed to go home. I got home, did my own homework, and went to bed. But I was pleased in my exhaustion; we had made real strides that night.

Sunday gathering. Starting that breakfast meeting (with eight youth, grades nine, ten, and eleven) with an explanation of "why a parable is power-filled," Lynn (intentionally with one team person present) was interrupted by my arrival. As I stood at the end of the room, both Sally and Lynn attacked me with pillows, beating me down to the carpet. Wearing a sport coat, Brent, one of the tenth graders (intentionally arriving late) entered, saw me curled in a ball on the rug, pulled two dollar bills from his wallet, placed them near my outstretched hand, and walked on by, reading his newspaper. Then Sally and Lynn, deep in a discussion about school, entered. Seeing me, they stepped over me and walked on by. Pastor Jim, wearing his clerical robe, entered. Sprinkling me with "holy water," he also passed by. Finally Sally, carrying an ugly wooden cross, entered. Leaning the cross against the wall so that it could stand, Sally carried me to the couch where several people made room for me to lie down. At that point Lynn read the parable of the good Samaritan, Luke 10:24-37. Lynn spoke to us about this parable. She pointed out that this parable would be outrageous in Jesus' day because the priest and Levite were the "good" people of society while the Samaritan was considered to be "scum." In Jesus' parable the "good" people walk on by, while the "bad" person proved himself to be truly "good."

I then posed four questions: (1) What common everyday things or experiences is Jesus talking about here? (2) How did Jesus twist around these things to give the parable meaning? (3) What was it about Jesus's life, do you suppose, that led him to tell this parable? (4) How does this parable connect with us and challenge us today? Working on newsprint with Sally as recorder, we discussed the questions and then restructured this parable as a present-day experience, telling it like this:

> A religious lawyer tried to trip Jesus by asking him how to get to heaven. Jesus asked him to give his interpretation. The professional said, "Love God totally and in the same way love your neighbor." Jesus said, "That is right." But the pro tried to cop out. He asked Jesus, "Who is my neighbor?" Jesus said, "This guy was going from the shopping center to the ghetto and these big dudes jumped him. They heisted everything they could use. When they left he was totally wiped out. A minister went by, saw the guy, but said, 'I don't want to get involved,' and drove on. In a few minutes a businessman in a new Caddie zoomed by, but he didn't want to get involved either.

Then a big greaser in an old junker saw the guy and said, 'Man, this cat is really wiped out.' He took the guy who had been mugged to a doctor. He paid the doctor and told him if it cost more he'd be willing to help out." Then Jesus asked the teacher of the law which one was a neighbor to the mugged guy. The lawyer said, "The greaser, of course." Jesus said, "You go and live the same way."

After confirmation breakfast we went across the lawn to church. This week we all ushered. Then we listened while Mr. Katzwinkle, chair of the Governing Board, and Pastor Jim engaged in a dialogue sermon on "The Parables of the Dominion." Most of us helped serve coffee and cookies in the "Second Phase Feedback," a discussion and coffee time following worship.

Thursday team meeting. That Thursday, team evaluation of the "good Samaritan" process design was positive. The new version, rewritten in class January 12 (see above), was ready to be shared in worship January 19. Agreeing to work with one eighth grader who was to read the rewritten parable, I suggested that person be Jason and that he rehearse the reading with me on Saturday. Because the film *Parable* had arrived early in the mail, Pastor Jim suggested that it be previewed in order to determine if the process we were planning thus far would work. After seeing the film, a series of matching questions was added, but we agreed that the clown white-marking process offered last week by Lynn would be perfect.

Suggesting that everyone who entered worship might "become clowns" with greasepaint during the reading of the good Samaritan, Lynn now argued for more involvement while both Sally and Jim urged caution. I stated that using clowns in the adult worship service too quickly could alienate a lot of people, and we decided not to go that route.

Considering Lynn's interest in actually "clowning" in church, Jim directed the team forward to February 2 and "popsicle puppets." Sally, wanting to organize the puppet workshop, indicated she had already located a craft shop supplier and an ample amount of material. Sally also reminded us of the role we had agreed to play in the church-sponsored Adolescent Health Fair on the last Sunday afternoon this month. This was a community information-sharing event during which twenty groups (including someone from a foster home, a doctor's group specializing in adolescent medicine, and the school-appointed drug intervention team) would set up display/conversation areas around the edges of fellowship hall, while several panels and individual presentations would occur near the front. We were responsible to "carry the message" to both the middle- and high-school crowd. Sally had designed a catchy flier; we agreed to hand it out and post it in the crucial areas where we felt folks would see (and read) it. We decided to see if we could post fliers in school. The meeting ended when my friend Matt arrived to take both myself and Lynn to the basketball game.

Sunday gathering. When January 19 rolled around, I was sure Jason (our reader of the rewritten parable) would forget and not show, and so I almost forgot the doughnuts, but Sally double-checked me, so food was being served as everyone arrived. Lynn had planned ahead and arrived in clown costume. Moving around the room, she quickly dabbed each cheek with bright greasepaint as the movie projector was set up. After viewing *Parable* we worked on the story line. Then we tried to name the most powerful scenes and who the characters were. Our discussion finally centered on one question: "Does resurrection in this film mean *we* become Christ figures?" We played with that idea for awhile, and then Lynn pulled us into our circle and, moving from person to person, touched each of us on the forehead with white clown makeup while saying, "God loves you; Christ frees you; go forth in love." We "went forth in love" to church, and Amy, one of the confirmation breakfast group, read the Old Testament lesson, "Am I My Brother's Keeper," from Genesis 4. An adult lay leader then read Luke 10:29-37, and eighth grader Jason presented what we had called our "contemporary reading" of the good Samaritan. It was well received.

Critical Reflection on the Model

The *covenant* holds, in part, when cross-age mentors (Sally, David, Lynn, and Pastor Jim) walk with youth into the experience of the faithful community. Pastor Jim introduces the rich resources of the faith, and models with the confirmation team how faithful members critically minister and reflect upon life experiences together. Brent, a tenth grader, is pulled into the teaching process, and David, a staffer, checks on Jason and in turn is checked upon by Sally. Patterns of care and concern pervade this breakfast gathering. One can claim that in "the breaking of bread" represented by sharing doughnuts, Jesus is embodied. God's human face takes shape as cross-age mentors share from their lives with younger persons as they reflect upon owning the covenant.[4]

The *tradition*, in this context, avoids most hierarchical connotations. There are adults present, but David has a real role to play with this team, and Jason, an eighth grader, also gets involved. Coming to "know" is a shared, interactive, experiential process connecting with the participant's reality. To "own" the tradition, confirmands are invited into the story and offered a way to experience the claims made by the story and to retell (and make proclamation in worship) the story *in their own words*. The good Samaritan *lives* when the "big greaser in the old junker" cares (surprise) for the person who had been "jumped" and "totally wiped out."[5]

The *pilgrimage* is not an afterthought for this confirmation gathering. Older spiritual guides ritually touch confirmands on the forehead, marking and claiming them while saying, "God loves you; Christ frees you; go forth in love." This is not a private, exclusive, spiritual club. There is a regularized call to service and to worship as part of the *Laos* (the "people of God"). This church, this "household" of God, makes room in worship for all of God's "householders," including its youth. Thus David's testimony of how, over the years, he had started ushering, moved to scripture reading, was challenged to participate within a dialogue sermon, and ultimately called to preach one summer Sunday, suggests the practice of *hospitality* on the part of the congregation for "the long haul."[6]

Ministry within the congregation is not the sole property of Pastor Jim. It is claimed by those accepting the congregation's charge to serve as confirmation team members. It is also an ongoing involvement of the congregation. Two specific occasions of ministry outside the congregation are mentioned by David. One concerns a vaccination trip into Central America in which doctors, nurses, and a youth known by David participated. The second is the adolescent health fair sponsored by the congregation and held in the church's fellowship hall. Both occasions are connected to the identity of the congregation and its professional, middle-class makeup. But the connection makes its own claim, that ministry is something connected to *our* reality: we minister as doctors; we are aware of and focus on adolescent health needs. Something powerful is modeled when gatekeepers not only open the door to being middle class but also understand what they do as Christian *vocation*.[7]

Summary

In summary, confirmation is envisioned as a *mentoring process* into the faithful community, as an *experiential immersion* within the story and vision of that community, as a *spiritual journey* of the faithful, and as an *initiation into a lifelong vocation* embodying *ministry*. As such, it reflects and incarnates the theological identity of the congregation. In another context, the editor of this book commented on how youth "connect" with a faithful church as they engage in the process of *becoming* and *belonging*:

> Here then is the difference for us who respond to this Exodus tale of Yahweh and a little band of people: youth who travel without such words and symbols, without such images and stories, travel without Yahweh and thus travel with faulty maps. They have no real food and no real guide. They are on journeys that often offer death-worlds instead of life-worlds. The community of faith, the people of god, the church, the keepers of the story of Yahweh and this little band, might consider the implications for living out this story with youth, of providing frameworks wherein . . . youth and trusted adults can depthfully explore the meaning of this story as it is played out within their context.[8]

CHAPTER FOUR

Pastor Jim's Strategy

In every age the community of faith must discover the
shape of its ministry.

James Whitehead and
Evelyn Eaton Whitehead
Method in Ministry

A pastor who is responsible for a small church confirmation program faces unique problems. As such, I have limited resources in terms of time and money, yet I want the young people to have the same sort of experience I had while growing up in a big church. That church provided me with caring adult leaders, a confirmation process relevant to my life, and a helpful entry into its adult practices. The relational style of that church buffered its bigness; I felt supported, cared for, and challenged. To this day, I can remember the names of the people who experienced that process with me. And I don't think that my experience should only occur in larger congregations; the pastoral ministry I believe I have with this small church demands that we—together—are very intentional about confirmation. I also wanted a set of experiences (like those described in chapters 7–10) that can be introduced by a confirmation team, implemented without a lot of time spent, that are economical to use, and that challenge young people.

As you can see from the previous chapter, I didn't use them as they are printed in this book. I did, however, hold several day-long planning meetings with the confirmation team during which I shared photocopies of several such experiences and spent time making each session "ours." Such a working process is not only exciting, it is also the critical way I taught the confirmation team. And because we used what we were planning to do with the confirmands, I expected that our shared journey would challenge us in ways we could not anticipate. I also wanted to combat the demeaning yet seductive role of popular culture by intentionally conveying in confirmation a community that demonstrates how the church can help us confront and interpret the values and expectations of our American culture; in other words, I wanted to share my small congregation's hope that confirmation should incorporate the confirmands into a faithful community.

It helps to know that I am not alone. Clearly, if I adopt a "Lone Ranger" style of leadership, I will burn out. Nevertheless, the economic clout of the bigger congregations often seems to orient the publishing houses to big church needs. Still, the average Protestant church in the United States is a smaller church (defined as having an average Sunday attendance of 150 or less), while the average church member is a member of a larger church (150 or more on a Sunday morning).[1] Thus most church adolescents will be engaged in confirmation within a large church, while most confirmation leaders will be involved in leading confirmation within a small church. This means that if you are a confirmation leader in a small church and reach out you will find that there are many other confirmation teachers close by within your denomination who are in the same boat as you are. You will also find that they are a ready source of information. They can share with you what is happening locally with respect to confirmation camps and workshops that help smaller churches occasionally have large confirmation group experiences. If there is nothing organized, however, they will often be eager to help you get one going. And they will typically be happy to share with you how they have handled some of those tough small-church questions. I believe that it is truly worth the effort to reach out and make those connections.

The Small Congregation

It is almost impossible to talk about the structure of confirmation in the small church without first considering some of the special dynamics of this type of congregation.[2] Even though we have spent a fair amount of time in this text helping you to come to grips with the fact that confirmation is no longer a rite of passage within our culture, you would never know it as you talk with the members of many smaller congregations. At least in my congregation, they believe they are a body of believers set apart. They are aware that the dominant culture doesn't often honor what they do, but for them, confirmation is a rite of passage into the family of the church. This clear identity strengthens the confirmation leader.

The small congregation is often defined by its members as one large, extended family. It is like a single-cell organism, where people know each other's life stories, even though there may be special cliques, inner circles, and power groups that threaten the unity of the family. Organisms like this are fairly careful about how they take newness into themselves and how it is assimilated. That carefulness is often expressed without conscious forethought. Thus, the strong identity gets communicated to youth in caring and occasionally noncaring ways. The "family story" of the church has consequences that must be faced by those who join. Such consequences come as a result of the weight of tradition.

A new minister attempting to challenge the sentiment, "We've always done it that way before," presents a threat to the unconscious sense of insider security that bonds the small church together. When confirmation has been "a class taught by the pastor" for as long as they can remember, the pastor who "reads the signs of the congregation" intuitively already knows, in the words of the early Americans, that reformers need to "tread lightly here." Yet, pastoral leadership also means, at least as I understand it, enacting some changes in the confirmation process. The way confirmation was structured in my congregation—as a "school"-only process—did not touch youth where they live. So I intentionally moved toward a new model with an old name.

The Model in the Pastor's Mind

The youth in my small church tend to be scattered across a variety of grades, as no one grade regularly has enough adolescents to form an age-graded confirmation community. Given this context, I hoped to be able to convince my congregation that confirmation was something other than school. I wanted to be intentional about designing something that concentrated upon teaching *tradition* preparatory to confirmation. I therefore concentrated on a preconfirmation church school program to pick up some older elementary children and the junior highs. It would run every year, culminating in a once-every-three-years confirmation experience that never resembled a class. So there is now a feeder program into confirmation in this small church that makes use of the Sunday school framework for junior highs and a once-every-three-years early Sunday morning confirmation class. I don't particularly care for the word *class* in conjunction with confirmation, but the confluence of all the above factors (including the word *class*) helped me negotiate my dilemma of having "to offer a class taught by the pastor on Sunday" while engaging in a fairly radical restructuring effort. That restructuring included a team approach for confirmation leadership, including one or two older youth, one or two adult sponsors, and myself.

I'm also aware that worship and service are the central practices of this community. Because of this, I planned never to have my confirmation meetings at the same time as common worship. We met in the manse before worship over breakfast. I did this because I wanted the confirmands to be involved strongly in the church's worship celebration. I also wanted to have mentors— adult persons who could connect to individual confirmands— readily available to tell the story of the faith, inviting the confirmands into more adult modes of being in this congregation (service is also an important part of ministry here.) So a Sunday morning confirmation breakfast, while unconventional, seemed to work precisely because of these considerations.

But even as I was beginning to restructure the confirmation program in this small church, I asked some of the older members how confirmation had been done in the past. This served two purposes. It helped the congregation feel that their traditions were heard, and it enabled me to catalog their expectations for confirmation. There is a great deal of literature about how to manage change in conflicted or power-blocked churches; however, just a word might be added about the resistance to change that the small congregation experiences. It can be a strength as well as a weakness. Small churches rarely throw the baby out with the bath water. They may be slow to change, but they can change. They respond best to planned change where they have a chance to minimize the risks involved before they implement the plan. They will resist impulsiveness not on the merits of the ideas but on the fact that change feels threatening and is therefore stressful. Do not take it personally. Slow down, try it again with planned change, and you will find that for the most part they resist the feeling and not the content.

Engaging in the long-term process of listening to stories about confirmation in this congregation, I began to sort out their unspoken expectations. Here are some examples: "But the pastor always teaches confirmation." "We always confirm the class on [fill in the blank] Sunday." "The class always meets on [fill in the blank] day." "We always test the confirmands on the [fill in the blank] rule of faith before they are confirmed." These expectations and others like them fall into an initial category of "How the Confirmation Program is Understood by the Larger Congregation." These expectations are hard to change because they are held in common by most of the adults of the congregation.

A second set of expectations, however, had to do more with the confirmands themselves: the curricula to use, the place of the meeting, the format of the experiences to be shared, the age (grade) of the confirmands, and so on. Here the church's elders were more willing to listen to a rationale that showed a new model was in the best interests of the young people. I found myself asking, particularly regarding this second set of expectations, "What does this church believe our youth really need?" Central to my reflection is that in the small church youth are joining a family that believes, in spite of what culture assumes, that confirmation will bring the confirmand within this family. Given this assumption, my hunch is that adolescents will therefore need to be part of an interpretive group (of youth and adult church members) that tries to make sense out of the claims presented by both the culture and the church. I therefore believe the challenge *for the congregation* is to provide a confirmation structure in which the youth and the congregation are jointly affirmed and respected even as they wrestle with what the faith means in today's world.

A Three-Phase, Multi-Year Confirmation Experience

Given all these factors, what actually occurred was a three-phase, multi-year experience:

Preconfirmation I *was a one-year church school-type classroom program taught by one lay person under the direction of the minister. The curricula focused on the people and stories of the Old Testament using themes that are foundational to the Christian story, i.e., concepts of covenant, election, God's working in history, revelation, prophecy, etc. This intentionally used a school format.*

Preconfirmation II, *was also a one-year church school-type classroom program taught by one lay person under the direction of the minister. The curricula here focused on the people and stories of the New Testament using themes that are foundational to the Christian story in such a way as to prepare for the confirmands experiential integration, i.e., concepts of baptism, Last Supper, grace, miracle, parable, crucifixion, resurrection, etc. This also intentionally used a school format.*

Confirmation *was a one-year youth breakfast club-type program led by a team of persons following the peer ministry model and including the minster, two older youth, and one or more adult sponsors. This team regularly met every Thursday after school to plan what would be done with the confirmands. We used program offerings like those suggested in this volume. [see chapters 7–10.]*

As we progressed into the model we discovered that more members wanted to serve on the team than we believed should serve. The Church Leaders therefore developed, in addition to the confirmation team, a junior high team. We sense that this move eventually will provide every older youth with an intentional ministry opportunity.

We also worked toward including several additional components in the confirmation process which, we felt, would expand the traditional classroom walls:

(1) A retreat program where confirmands get away at least twice a year for an overnight. This might include going to confirmation camp in the summer or special confirmation rallies.

(2) A youth program where confirmands meet at least monthly in order to play together.

(3) Inclusion in our stewardship program where confirmands would be asked to give of their time, i.e., CROP walks, work trips, medical events like those noted by David, and cleanup days at the church.

(4) An intentional sponsor program will be central to the confirmation process. Worship attendance with sponsors will occasionally result in postchurch reflection meals.

These additional components were essential for a number of reasons. They helped integrate the story and the vision with lived church experience and helped the young person engage in a crossgenerational Christian community. The confirmands' enhanced sense of becoming and belonging and interaction with older Christians allowed them to become a part of this small church's covenantal ministry.

Critical Reflection on the Model

No model is perfect. Certainly Pastor Jim's model is not meant to fit all congregations. Nevertheless, this model does address several concerns. One concern is that confirmands often come to the confirmation program with a wide variety of backgrounds with respect to their knowledge of the stories of the faith. Some have been to church school since they were small, while others arrive with little Christian education background. Almost universally, however, their parents see value in confirmation that they did not see in the traditional church school class. This is often frustrating for the confirmation leader who is working to integrate conceptual knowledge with lived experience while finding that half of the group has not been exposed to the tools of the tradition. This structure allows, however, for emphasis on more traditional content during the preconfirmation phases, and since those phases are under the auspices of a church that still accepts church school as being of value, attendance tends to be better.

A second concern, the sparse numbers of youth often found in the small church, is also addressed. Confirmation in this context is intentionally offered every third year. This action avoids the feeling that "we aren't having confirmation this year." It also allows for interaction between different laity and the young people over a longer period of time. Lay persons teach the first two phases and then work as sponsors during the third. This also gives the program and the pastor a broad base of support in the congregation.

A final concern, yet a very important one, that the pastor not burn out, is clearly addressed by this model. With lay persons playing key roles, it allows for a very full confirmation experience without overloading the pastor's schedule. The peer ministry model from which Pastor Jim has borrowed is congruent with the values undergirding his small church. Everyone has a role to play within this congregation, and if a confirmation process is thought to become more lively with several people helping out, why not try it? Pastor Jim recognizes how well this approach fits the small church he serves. He states, "These folks are family. They may resist some things, but they aren't dumb, and when kids are putting a number one priority on confirmation attendance, believe me, adults notice." Pastor Jim also notes one other interesting happening:

> Before we began this process, this church had been in existence eighty years without anyone being ordained from its membership. Currently we have three people actively considering the ordained ministry, and I know it's because of experience they had on the confirmation team. Even if they don't get ordained, their lay ministry will continue. And the family that this little church prides itself on being will not be the same again. We've changed.

Summary

The small church experience is still normative for the majority of churches in America. This holds a great deal of joy as well as frustration for those pastors who minister within that context.

However, once one recognizes that the small church is often structured like an extended family and not like the rest of corporate America, as many larger churches tend to be, then the dilemmas, the rewards, and the benefits are many and varied. Confirmation, understood as a churchly rite of incorporation, can be one such rewarding experience. And the team model may provide one framework that makes sense, pragmatically and theologically, for such congregations.

CHAPTER FIVE

A Confirmation Colloquy

Youth need to be visible in the life of the church, not
relegated to a corner of the church school wing.
Ginny Ward Holderness
Youth Ministry: The New Team Approach

What follows is an edited transcript of a conversation between the six contributors to this book. At the time of this discussion, Brenda Kinder served as a director of Christian education; Gary Halstead, Richard Kirchherr, and Richard Wolf served as associate pastors; Timothy Nelson served as an interim pastor; and William Myers served as the academic dean of a seminary. All have extensive experience in leading confirmation programs. The conversation centers on the future of confirmation, and this initial segment reflects concerns regarding the church's historic emphasis upon confirmation as a school-like class.

The Models of Confirmation

BILL: What do you folks think about Pastor Jim and David's strategy for confirmation?

GARY: I envy them. Currently in my setting, confirmation occurs on Sunday morning as a kind of class taught by some very good lay people, but I only get involved with confirmands in the three retreats we hold with them each year.

BILL: Are you challenged by David and Jim?

GARY: Yes. I strongly relate to what they are suggesting. Ours is a small church setting, and were we to offer the actual confirmation experience every three years, we ought to be able to guarantee a critical mass.

45

RICH: Except for size, my context is very similar to the one pre-
          sented by Pastor Jim and David. For twenty to thirty
          ninth-grade confirmands each year, we commission a
          confirmation staff of two adults, three senior highs, and
          myself. We have weekly staff meetings; confirmation oc-
          curs weekly after school; and we require Sunday wor-
          ship attendance.

BRENDA: Our context doesn't look anything like Pastor Jim's. Con-
          firmation is for eighth graders, occurs with the pastor
          every Sunday after morning worship, but only lasts for
          thirteen weeks. We conclude with a one-day retreat that
          emphasizes the spiritual pilgrimage.

KIRCH: In my setting, the two core conditions of tradition and
          covenant are emphasized. The confirmation experience
          occurs between our two worship celebrations every Sun-
          day for a year, concluding with a mandatory work camp.

RICH: Work camp is required?

KIRCH: It is. The confirmands form the bulk of the work camp-
          ers, but enough youth from the youth group and adults
          from the church go to integrate the confirmands into the
          church in a very pragmatic way. Work camp bridges
          confirmands into the working ministry of the church.

BILL: So the congregations represented in this colloquy offer
          different confirmation frameworks and, I take it, see
          some challenges to their practice as they compare/con-
          trast what they do with what David and Pastor Jim do?

KIRCH: Exactly. We bridge into the congregation, out of a sense
          of covenant and vocation, but we aren't as comfortable
          with pilgrimage or spiritual talk. We need to consider
          what that means—both for us and our youth.

GARY: And while we're more comfortable with pilgrimage and
          tradition, we don't do a good job bridging youth into the
          ministry practices of the congregations. Adults inten-
          tionally limit the ways youth can get involved. We are
          weak in passing on the covenant and integrating youth
          into the church.

RICH: Maybe I'm just missing it, but I think all four core condi-
          tions are present in my context. If pushed I'd say we are
          strongest with teaching the tradition and bridging youth

into the ministry and practice of the congregation. We are weaker with spirituality (pilgrimage) and covenant. But they are still present.

BRENDA: Ditto. We're solid on teaching the tradition and bringing youth into the ongoing ministry practices of the congregation. We're weak in pilgrimage and covenant. Not many adults want to mentor adolescents or share their own faith journey.

BILL: Let me observe that all of you mentioned tradition, or teaching, as something you felt was done well in your setting. Any comments?

RICH: The obvious comment, to me, is that confirmation has been conceived of as a class in the Protestant tradition.

GARY: And has been assigned to the pastor.

BILL: Resulting in more attention being paid to content and not as much attention being paid to process?

BRENDA: I think that's right. It's kind of like the only place where a parent expects their child to have one-to-one contact with the pastor. And that kind of contact tends to be equated, at least in my context, with a regularized class.

RICH: It's like the parents have a long tradition of saying, "This is my last chance to plug Junior into faith, morality, values, whatever." So Junior gets sent to the pastor. And the pastor becomes one more principal faced by the adolescent.

BILL: The pastor, on the other hand . . .

RICH: . . . suddenly faces a class filled with squirming adolescents, many of them not known by the pastor, and some who are downright hostile. To set up the pastor in this way is unfair, but most of us do the classroom thing out of reflexive habit. In some perverse way, we try to emulate what happened to us in seminary. And it does not work.

Dueling Cultures of Meaning

GARY: Let's see, I've taught eight confirmation groups now, and I'd estimate that at least 40 percent of the confirmands who arrived at the first organizational meeting were stepping into church for the first time. The first time ever. Their parents weren't involved on any regular basis, but because this was confirmation, all of a sudden these youth were to be involved. This was a command performance. They did the year-long confirmation program, were confirmed, and then immediately became inactive.

RICH: I think, for those parents, confirmation is understood to be a last ditch infusion; i.e., if the kids go to confirmation, maybe it will "take." The unfortunate thing is that if they (and their parents) haven't been part of the congregation before confirmation, it will be very difficult for them to become part of the congregation after confirmation.

KIRCH: I agree. I also see a lot of what I call first-timers. It's their first time in church, and I find myself asking one of the youth I already know (because they have been active in church) to identify these people. I ask someone, "Who is that person? And that person over there? And there? And there?" I think it is very hard to impact people like this. They clearly catch a double message from their parents. I know they represent an opportunity, but everything mom and dad have communicated tends to cancel out that opportunity. So these are youth who are "just putting in hard time" in confirmation.

RICH: Parents are tremendously important regarding what happens, but I have seen these first-timers stay within the congregation as long as the church has active structures in place to challenge them with ministry and to encourage their involvement.

BRENDA: Unfortunately, if the parents don't participate in worship or the ministry of the church, these youth don't either, primarily because worship participation and active ministry on their part isn't understood by them as being necessary to be a member. Neither mom nor dad attends. Why, says the resistant youth, should I? So the kids prefer to come to something like youth fellowship; they avoid or ignore worship. That's why the core condition of pilgrimage gets shortchanged.

KIRCH: Part of this may be specific to our congregations, but I believe it is also specific to most mainline congregations. We don't have strong membership expectations regarding ministry or worship participation for adults, so it's understandable why youth stay away. The church doesn't challenge adults vocationally, so it isn't always connected to either the vocation or the ways lay people celebrate. Because this is true, it's also understandable why pilgrimage, or any spiritual language, is weak.

BRENDA: Parents see confirmation as the last moment they have to force their children to attend church. They will say to the child, "Do as I say, not as I do," and send that child for a last infusion of spirituality or of values before they give up. We did a written evaluation of all the parents of our confirmands two years ago. They clearly believed confirmation was a spiritual moment of reckoning. When there was no perceived increase of spirituality in 80 percent of the youth, the parent is willing to state, "Well, I've done all I can do; now it's up to them to decide where they stand regarding church." So I'm wondering, in this regard, if we aren't missing the real problem; i.e., the lack of involvement of the parents in the spiritual life of the congregation. [There is a general nodding of heads in agreement.]

BILL: Are you saying that confirmation doesn't work unless the congregation is faithful and accepts "me" as a first-class member?

RICH: It could be put that way, but it goes deeper. The issue is, "Does the church have an identity and a story it wants to pass on to another generation?"

GARY: Am I being cynical here, or isn't the deep, deep issue the fact that the church as a community of faith isn't too lively an option for the adults either?

KIRCH: Certainly it has to do with the adults and the expectations about ministry and pilgrimage we have of any member. I am often asked at confirmation workshops, "How can we keep them in the church?" But under that question is the deeper question Gary points at, namely, "Are the *adults* involved in ministry and in pilgrimage?"

BILL: Are you saying that all we need to do to "fix" confirmation is to get adults active in congregations and the youth naturally will follow? That seems simplistic to me.

GARY: I think that is simplistic. I believe adults enter churches, in part, because of their needs. They enter groups in which age is often a key factor. Here, with several age-mates, they have a "culture of meaning." To a certain extent they have constructed the church around these needs, and in a certain way, these adults are embedded in this culture. They want their kids to be embedded in the same culture of meaning, but the kids won't do that because they are already embedded in a different culture with their peers and contemporary American culture. Most studies show youth implicitly accept the values of their parents even as they explicitly reject them. But we don't offer many settings where we name or remotely deal with this. That's a part of why it's hard to find adults willing to mentor adolescents. It's tough work in this culture for anyone to mentor them.

BILL: And you are suggesting that the cultural tacit approval of the confirmand's parents is more powerful than any common community of faith idea?

GARY: I'm saying that, at the minimum, these parents have encouraged, have thrust these youth into the values of the contemporary culture. They want their kids to succeed in this culture, to be popular, to have good grades, to compete! And the kids do this; some of them do it very well. And this culture of meaning, generally speaking, is antagonistic to the common community of faith idea.

RICH: For example?

GARY: Think of what I'm calling two cultures of meaning, and then ask, "What about the different ways adults and youth value music and play? What about the ways people socially relate and their forms of entertainment? What about the way a youth experiences an event as worshipful in contrast to what adults understand as worship?" It's very different. Rarely do we discuss or deal with this difference in church. I don't think there is a conspiracy locking kids out of the adult concept of church. It's just that most adults mentor the claims of the culture and don't mentor the claims of the church.

Cross-Generational Leadership

KIRCH: Gary, I'm not sure I totally agree with what you are saying. You sound very pessimistic. You seem to be saying there are no spiritual adult role models in the faith. I want to say that I have this hope: that certain adult mentors, guides, or guarantors can be authentic to their own culture of meaning and yet serve as faithful living bridges for the church and for adolescents. I think adults who are involved in confirmation groups must be authentic adults, but they are more like elder brothers or older sister than anything else I can name, and they stand with youth in real ways.

RICH: Here we confess the human side of Christ as being as important as the divine side. Jesus waded through the waters as elder son; he stands with us. We want to have people who haven't closed down their lives, who are real in their adultness, involved with youth in spiritual confirmation experiences of depth. We want, in a deep way, to challenge both adult and adolescent cultures of meaning from within a community of faith. That's what Pastor Jim is for David and Lynn—he is a guarantor.

KIRCH: I like the phrase "adult Christian friend." This, to me, is a guide, i.e., an adult who has more lived experience than the adolescents and who is called to come back and stand with the youth. That's a good image for me.

BILL: In all of this, I hear you saying that we have to watch out for the seduction of being "just one of the kids" and joining their culture of meaning. Adults aren't youth.

GARY: I'd agree. And I know a number of adults who name this process by saying that I know who I am and where I stand and I will stand with you, but I will also confront and challenge you. That's part of who I am, too.

BILL: So . . . what about leadership here—team? One person? What is the age of these adults working with the confirmation community?

BRENDA: I believe one leader must assume responsibility for the overall direction of confirmation.

RICH: Normally this is a pastor.

BILL: And I agree, but I'd want that pastor to recruit some slightly older youth as well as some people of different ages to be involved with a leadership team; i.e., a variety of authentic adults who model, "I'm on a pilgrimage, and I'll share that with you." I really believe we must challenge churches with the four core conditions and the team idea. Churches that have confirmation with one leader are just plain missing the boat.

BRENDA: And I'd emphasize that people who are forty, fifty, and sixty need to be involved with this group. What an impact they would have! And I think the spiritual questions would get addressed. All ages, together. The intergenerational aspect is essential.

The Politics of Worship

[Conversation turned to confirmation as the moment in which *becoming* and *belonging* are placed within the claims of early baptismal vows.]

BRENDA: Parents push their kids toward the church, in part because they look at the church as a positive place that is safe. And with all the unsafe stuff that happens within the contemporary culture, parents push for church involvement. It's logical.

GARY: Agreed. But it is unfortunate when parents wait until this age arrives before they begin involving their youth in the church. I would argue that if we wait to begin at such a late point, we miss where the real connectors occur—in childhood. I think the church has to engage children very early. I believe that children in the elementary grades are accepting the messages of the church that either confirm or reject their becoming and belonging.

BILL: And we often block children from active participation in worship.

GARY: I think that's generally true.

RICH: We're going to get in trouble here. If we tell the readers of this book that the way to keep youth in the church is to involve them as children in the adult worship service—that's a loaded issue.

BILL: But if the church isn't a lively, dynamic place where a cross-generational response to God occurs in a regular way, then I question if any program, no matter how powerful, will make much sense. This statement translates into: "How, then, do we worship as a 'people of God'?"

GARY: And there's a hidden valuation in all of this. In the denominational church I represent, confirmation has to do with the confirming of one's baptismal vows, usually taken for adolescents when they were children. If confirmation is about generating a "meaning-making process" in relation to confirming one's baptismal vows, why the big emphasis on worship?

BILL: Because the church is a *community* of persons. This community "stands in" for God at the rite of confirmation. The community says yes to each individual's affirmation of their baptismal vows. Other rites may have a variety of criteria, but confirmation has about it a sense of commissioning into the ministry of a community.

KIRCH: And a part of the covenant is that this community—the church—will help these persons claim their spirituality. The church is saying that it has good news, but there are people who are not part of the church who are still very spirited people. That's fine, but this is about the active process of the church that helps in the naming and claiming of spirituality and ministry. The church has some helpful resources that impact what it means to live in this world.

BRENDA: Why, then, does confirmation usually occupy the church for a year or less? I know there are many models for confirmation and that some last three years, but the norm seems to be the academic, nine-month "year." And so, here we are—mentors, powerful issues of faith, spirituality, and ministry—all packed into nine months!

RICH: I'd argue for a strong, one-year program, but I'd also insist that structures leading into and out of that year be equally sturdy.

GARY: Exactly. Children ought to be involved in worship, and we need to extend the mentor process past the actual rite of confirmation. I'm aware of the irony connected with one church I served in that when youth joined the church their adult mentor's job ended, but when adults joined that same church, on that day sponsors stood with them, ready to integrate these adults into the faithful life of the church. Why not something ongoing like this for youth?

BILL: And you believe that the covenant is better honored when adult sponsors incorporate confirmands into the life of the worshipping congregation?

GARY: For me, the key ingredient is the mutual respectful way adults are covenantally present with confirmands. This means taking them seriously as members and heirs of the covenant. An absolute bottom line for me is that youth must sense that they are valued as persons in this church. They are part of "the household of God."

BILL: And here is where the church must honor its baptismal vows, that these confirmands are of worth because they equally are God's children. The rite of confirmation proclaims, from the church's side, that the covenant is a promise for the confirmand.

Telling the Story

[Talk moved into a consideration of *tradition* and how confirmands are or are not immersed within the rich resources of the faith-story.]

BRENDA: But what about the kid who has never been to church and who, at the insistence of mom and dad, shows up for the confirmation process?

BILL: That's a tough one for me.

BRENDA: The problem is that they don't have the same tools I've come to expect from those confirmands who have had a longer history of involvement with the church. In one sense these new youth have broader questions. In another, however, when we use words like spirituality and ministry, we have to discover where the person is located. These aren't words they recognize. Often this is real foggy.

RICH: Confirmation for such persons might be understood to be a conversion experience, and the mainline gets nervous when people talk about conversion in the church. I think I'm more in tune with confirmation as a process of spirituality, an ongoing pilgrimage. And I have to ask of this newcomer, "How, for you, does this walk take place? Do we walk side-by-side? Do I push from behind? Or can I engage the person as a spiritual guide?"

BILL: For that to occur, I'd hunch that some mentoring relationships must occur. No canned curricula can replace getting close on such a walk. There's a tremendous relational component to spirituality.

KIRCH: There are, in confirmation programs, opportunities for transformational experiences. I think, for me personally, that transformative experiences are often so in retrospect. I am aware of this issue as I intentionally structure what might occur, for example, on a retreat. Memory plays a key role here. I've had adults say that a retreat experience long ago is crucial now in their faith journey. This is a tremendous formational opportunity.

GARY: And, in that intentional sense, as we share the story, the mythos of our Christian heritage and tradition, such stories bring with them a richness of meaning that goes far beyond the actual moment. So, while this isn't indoctrinating in any harsh, prohibitive sense, we experience together the Christian story so that the confirmands acquire the tools necessary to unpack what Kirch is talking about—these transformational experiences. Here are the tools, we say, and they are helpful tools for your journey.

BILL: In our cultural invention of adolescence we have emphasized the idea of identity. This makes adolescence the most propitious time to reflect on earlier memories and current experiences, understanding these to be building blocks for an emergent faith stance. This may be one of the few times adults intentionally take time to listen, reflect, and comment on this process in an active, caring way. The adolescent says, "See what I am *becoming*. Help me with my becoming." When the church doesn't provide the adolescent with the tools of the tradition, a time for reflection on the memory-building transformative experiences, and mentoring adults who actively enter this process, it backs away from the absolutely critical faith moment in the becoming process of adolescence.

RICH: We can challenge their faith stance and critically impact their becoming in powerful ways. We do this by how we structure the confirmation process.

BILL: And challenge makes a positive twist on the old use of "conversion." We can directly challenge adolescents by immersing them in the story and still being supportive in the critical reflection such a challenge brings to them. We, the church, need to provide adolescents with powerful experiences, tools, and caring processes of reflection. If we don't do this, we've abdicated our calling.

GARY: I want to argue that such a process as we are discussing here won't occur if confirmation is only framed as "schooling."

KIRCH: But school is only pejorative in confirmation when the only place we meet is a classroom and one adult is the authority in charge. To teach doesn't necessarily mean that we are in such a lock-step mode. In a large church context, the class designation helps identify where they fit within the structure. I use the word *class* as representative of a learning place, and I want to see such usage as positive. But I also agree with you; confirmation class isn't like school.

RICH: I disagree with you. I think any use of the word *class* is equated by youth to the school experience where they exist Monday through Friday. I personally believe the church experience is qualitatively different from class. I try to stay away from any use of the word *class*, and I am intentional in the use of the word *group*, as in "confirmation *group*."

KIRCH: What do you use in place of *teacher*?

RICH: I prefer *leader* or *pastor.*

GARY: Is confirmation an example of religious *education?* Or is confirmation more like learning a way of life?

RICH: Yes.

GARY: Both?

RICH: Yes, but I fear that we do a better job with number one, education, and avoid number two, a way of life. Let me put it this way. I fully expect that many persons will take the numerous "experiences" we've included in this book and use them as "lesson plans" in "classrooms."

BILL: How is that a bad thing?

RICH: To learn a way of life we struggle together, and so these are markers for us, but only if they help us critically reflect on our experience as a people of faith. That's not a *classroom* definition of confirmation; it's a *pilgrimage* definition.

The Presence of the Holy Spirit

[The discussion moved again to center around *pilgrimage* as the spiritual journey of the faithful individual.]

BILL: What's the "glue" of the covenant?

GARY: As the adults have respect for each youth's spiritual pilgrimage, they join with that youth's lived experience. This stance is different from demanding that the youth come into their—the adult's—lived experience. When adults can stand with youth in this way, then youth are able and willing to do the reverse. But I believe adults must make the initial move. Sharing the experience of pilgrimage, and all that implies, is the glue of the covenant.

RICH: We've talked for quite awhile without mentioning God or Jesus Christ or the Holy Spirit, and I think that we— the mainline congregations—do this too often. The glue is the faith of the youth and the adult in an actual communication between the two. If it isn't real, then it's just empty words. And we can't manipulate this, because the Holy Spirit is involved.

GARY: The Holy Spirit cannot—and I agree with you in this—be programmed. Does that invalidate the intentional thought—all the words which might be called "programs" or "lesson plans" by some folks—that fill this book?

RICH: We *invoke* the Holy Spirit, but that doesn't guarantee the presence of the Holy Spirit. And I don't knock our intentional experiences. No one ever said that the Holy Spirit was opposed to intentional religious practice. But we can't *control* the Holy Spirit.

BRENDA: Yet, if we are honest, a lot of the confirmands won't understand talk about the Holy Spirit. They aren't all at the same stage of the journey of faith. Many don't understand the language of faith, and it's a real problem we cannot avoid. We have to honestly interact where they are, not where we want them to be.

KIRCH: Let me try to bridge this. I think Brenda and Rich are talking about the same thing, but we need to tie what they say to each other. I think we must use the language of faith; we also need to be honest with the fact that to many youth such talk is a foreign language. But we're committed to the idea that these words house resources from our tradition that we believe could be powerful and important for these youth. At the same time we hope to connect with the experience of where each youth is located in order to nurture and challenge them even as they begin to understand this language. The traditional language, if we stick with it, gives them tools to talk about something that often is very difficult to name.

RICH: So that when, after a communion service on a work camp in which we actually washed each other's feet, one youth says to me, "That was awesome, a real rush."

KIRCH: I may respond, "Yeah, the Holy Spirit was present with us!"

BRENDA: But what about the kid who doesn't get the "rush" and who can't connect to your words, Kirch, and who is still asked to commit?

GARY: We can't program these kids, but if we believe the Holy Spirit is present in our experience of life, then we intentionally engage in a kind of invocation when we enter certain moments together. We call on God to be present, and we frame our call in language we believe to be helpful for the youth in our contextual situation. I don't think this is "programming."

RICH: Yeah. And John (who says, "I don't get it") also experiences the response of Susan (who says, "Awesome"). It's a communal connection that's also made. Being "religious" gets connected to the communal response as well as the individual pilgrimage.

KIRCH: I think that's highly appropriate. Part of the power of the biblical story is that it witnesses to how God impacts the lives of other people. As Susan witnesses to John, so too can we affirm the biblical witness as one that points to God's ongoing impact in the lives of persons just like us. How many times do we ask people to inhabit the biblical stories, to step inside them and try them on for size. We know that in reality these stories are the stories of our lives. That's what Susan is saying to John: something connects here.

BILL: Stepping into such stories equips us for the journey.

RICH: The leaders must be genuine in all this.

BRENDA: It's that honesty, modeled by caring adults, that could encourage John to say, "Hey, I didn't get it. Help me!"

Marginalized Members

[Finally, the talk turns to the "forever" struggle (the "politics") of confirmation.]

BRENDA: It's a "forever struggle" to have the adults believe that youth have value in other ways than merely setting up tables for potluck dinners.

BILL: The totality of Christian service is to be found (disbelief) in setting up tables?

BRENDA: Yes. It's a real struggle to get youth equated with being part of the ministry of the whole church. They are second-class citizens in their own church, and they know it.

RICH: Let's be honest here. The church is a political institution like every other human institution. If you assume total leadership of confirmation without involving other powerful adults who have connections in the structures of the congregation, you should expect to become a marginalized program.

BILL: You intentionally invite these folks into the confirmation process?

RICH: Exactly. Into the group experiences, the confirmation retreat, and on all the occasions when we do intergenerational exchanges. Youth also make presentations in all the adult power places. If you are intentional about this, things change.

BRENDA: Your comments are helpful. But I am angry that youth are often held to higher standards. Let one fire extinguisher be discharged in the building, and watch the reaction of the adults.

RICH: I'm a political advocate for youth. f a tenth of what we talk about in this book is true, confirmation needs to confront and challenge the adult members of the congregation with reality. We just cannot afford to marginalize youth and the experience of confirmation. The church must have a higher vision.

BILL: I'm aware that in another age those whom we today call "adolescent" were birthing children, shouldering the plow, and settling our nation. Today we say, "Wait until you grow up," but I've been in settings of ministry where youth ministered better than most adults.

BRENDA: I agree. In order for the church to have this higher vision Rich talks about, it must engage in ministry. And when it does, youth ought to be present, too.

BILL: I'm aware that there are about sixty years of youth ministry among those gathered for this colloquy, and while that doesn't make this a better statement, I want to claim what you say as emerging from the shared experience of those many years of ministry with adolescents, adults, and confirmation. Thank you.

CHAPTER SIX

Youth, Spirituality, and the Church

...the Bible invites us to join in and to participate in the
ongoing pilgrimage of those who live in the shattering of
history, caring in ways which matter, secured by the covenanting God *who is likewise on pilgrimage in History.*

Walter Brueggemann
The Bible Makes Sense

A young child learning to walk pulls upright, grasps the edge of a
table, and leans toward an adult hand stretched from a nearby
chair. For just a moment, the child determinedly teeters forward in
almost a first step and then tumbles to the floor, but, chortling in
glee, rises to begin the process again.

Philip Phenix, writing about moments such as these, notes
that the child was engaging in a "curriculum of transcendence."[1]
"Transcending" suggests stepping over, around, or through every
real or imagined condition limiting the fullest expression of what
we are created to be. While God, the "transcendent one," limit-
lessly transcends, we who are created in God's image know deep
inside that we are created for more than merely crawling, and it is
spirit, according to Phenix, that sends a child chortling in glee, back
to the table and the outstretched hand, ready to engage in the process of transcendence again, and again, and again.

A Curriculum of Transcendence

Phenix suggests that every person is engaged in just such an
ongoing spirited curriculum of transcendence; this is, he claims,
the basic ongoing dynamic of human living. It is inherently religious, and everyone engages in the same process of transcendence

61

whether or not a person affirms or rejects the dogma or formal components of organized religion often used to interpret and name the experience of transcendence. Like John Dewey, Phenix wanted to affirm the "religious" while understanding "religion" as more properly suggestive of formal and abstract cumulative traditions.[2]

The authors of this book belong to the Christian church—one of those cumulative traditions. Although not all religions value transcendence, this tradition does, and it identifies "spirit" as that which empowers a person or a community as it engages in the communal process of transcendence. Christian spirituality is anchored deep within these dynamics as the emerging way people of the tradition who are engaged in transcendence have begun to name and interpret that process. And the Holy Spirit is the ongoing activity and presence of a God who creates, invites, and even lures us within this process.

Wading in the Water

Can we describe what this looks like? With the child or youth who stands at the edge of their knowing in the presence of a caring peer or adult, there is a moment occasioned by the invitation of transcendence when the child or youth is at the edge of their very being. And they take the step—"wade into the waters"—and transcend, spiritedly, themselves or their circumstances. The Russian theoretician, L. S. Vygotsky, calls "wading into the waters" the occasion when one enters a "zone of proximal development."[3] It is proximal because a caring peer or adult stands with the child or youth in an overlapping experiential transcending moment. It is developmental because it involves a passage. It suggests that the caring human (or adult, teacher, peer, or religious educator) who stands with the learner at that moment of passage (that proximal moment) can intentionally provide "scaffolding" to help the person negotiate this developmental task.

Vygotsky's zone of proximal development and our use of the word *scaffolding* are helpful as we begin to describe and understand how we might intentionally approach the experience of confirmation. But whatever words from whatever disciplines we use to name this process, we want to emphasize a proactive stance toward confirmation that recognizes the importance of experience.

Youth in Church

Unfortunately, when we contemplate the actual presence of youth in church and the reality of many confirmation programs, we must recognize, for the most part, that the implications of transcendence for this age and the necessary conditions for a spirited engagement with confirmands are not in place. What we have instead are age-graded divisions mimicking the public school with a resultant confirmation model that is not structured as a community of faith reflecting on the experience of transcendence. For the most part the church rarely ministers to or with youth who are—of necessity—already engaged in a spirited dialogue with the transcendent invitations life has extended to them. Unfortunately, the result of having abandoned the field is that the curriculum of transcendence has come, at least for adolescents within this country, to be driven by other cultural metaphors and visions.[4] Normatively, within the church, an adolescent engaged in confirmation:

(1) will not be an active participant or insider in the worship gatherings of the faithful except for token "youth Sundays";
(2) will have no vote and no role in the actual governance of the youth program or the adult structure of the church;
(3) will never be challenged or nurtured by adult mentors into any faithful form of Christian ministry; and
(4) will, as a result of these and other similar factors, come to believe that things religious, spiritual, or of consequence to their lives are never discussed or acted upon in real ways within their local church.

We can also say that there are exceptions to this pattern. Pastor Jim and confirmation staff member David's testimony in Chapters 3 and 4 demonstrate that it does not have to be this way. It is unfortunate to note, however, that their thoughtful approach to confirmation clearly is an exception.

Becoming Intentional

In order for the governing bodies of a congregation to call forth the vocational gifts of youth, they must first be aware of what those gifts are, and that it is, indeed, vital for every congregation to include youth in every aspect of the church's life. Using the four ways to evaluate a confirmation program (noted in chapter 2) is a start, but this is not always an easy task. Churches tend to be set in their ways and still cling to a cultural understanding of adolescents as unqualified for certain roles and responsibilities in the life of the church. And, if the youth do not see a particular level of commitment as being important to their confirmand status, they also may not have the desire to be involved. In such a discussion, it is helpful to lean on the biblical theology of covenant. In many churches, covenanting often only takes place at the level of financial stewardship. But confirmands may be intentionally asked to covenant in areas of worship attendance, giving, attending youth fellowship groups, and many other areas of the ministering church in which the youth has interest or in which the congregation needs additional help. (A sample "New Member's Covenant" may be found in the resource appendix. Please keep in mind that covenanting is not the same as "contracting," as all new members have choices as to how involved they wish to be in church. Covenanting in this intentional sense, however, adds a dimension of commitment to one's promises made at the time a confirmand enters the membership of this church.)

The church that wants to confront this issue ought to be intentional about involving newly confirmed youth within (1) existing youth groups, (2) church leadership, (3) ministry/ service, and (4) worship.

Including youth in existing youth groups. Often a youth's primary covenanting experience of the church is through a church's fellowship groups (youth groups). If a church does not already have such youth groups for those in confirmation, often it starts such involvement after confirmation. In some congregations this is understood to be a natural progression, and adolescents see participation in youth fellowship as the next logical step following confirmation. In some congregations, however, confirmation ends, and youth never find a way to participate either in the church or in the youth group. This is where the break-away point occurs for many churches. However, if there is no logical break between the moment of confirmation and ongoing involvement in church and in the youth group, all youth who are newly confirmed may feel the lure to move into the welcoming church and the existing youth group structure. The time immediately following confirmation thus becomes logical for the welcoming and celebrating to occur. Just as the congregation welcomes the youth into the church at the time of confirmation, youth fellowship groups may also provide special times of welcoming. A "welcome the confirmands" party or picnic, a "welcoming overnighter," or a "community-building retreat" are all possibilities here (see chapter 7, "Focus Event"). Such activities say to youth that they are important to the life of the congregation, and the sooner such a message is conveyed, the better. These special welcoming occasions, however, should not merely be announced in a letter, flier, or poster. Personal invitations work better than publicity. Ask the older members of the youth group and the adult youth sponsors to contact several of the confirmands by phone or in person. This says that someone cares; the church is "embodied" or "incarnated" by such persons.

Church leadership. Many youth serve on committees in their clubs, out-of-school organizations, or student governments. Why should the church be any different? Youth should be invited to serve on the various committees, structures, councils, and boards which are important in leading the church on the local, regional, and national levels. Important decisions are made here, and if baptism means that we "all are God's children" and is held up as a Christian principle, then every segment of the congregation should have representation on the various governing bodies. In this regard, we must not forget that youth represent a good-sized fraction of most congregations.

Service. Members of the church serve others in a variety of ways. Youth should be encouraged to participate in the forms such service takes as well, whether ushering or running the audio system during worship or delivering "meals on wheels" to homebound folks. Note how Pastor Jim (chapter 4) involved youth in the ministry of the confirmation team. (Again, please refer to the

"New Member's Covenant" for further ideas.) This possibility for intentional ministry is determined by a particular church's identity; no two churches minister in exactly the same ways. But a church, to be faithful, engages in *diakonia*, the ministry of service, and youth who are in the process of considering membership must be involved in such ministry.

Worship. The "work of the people" (liturgy) involved in worshipping God requires many participants, each with necessary roles to play. This is the occasion to clarify the adolescent's response to God. The involvement of youth in the worship experience may take many forms. Reading scripture (and other lay-liturgist tasks), serving as acolytes or greeters, serving communion, singing in the choir, offering instrumental music, and yes, even preaching at times other than the once-a-year "youth Sunday." Youth have important contributions to make in worship.

Summary

Confirmands hear that when they are confirmed, they are to assume full membership in the church of Jesus Christ. By encouraging the involvement of newly confirmed youth in all areas of the congregational life, the congregation shows that it means what it says. But this is a two-way street. Through the confirmand's participation in the various areas of the church each youth gains new insight into what it means to be a church member, but there are both rights and responsibilities associated with membership. Service in the practice of ministry in the church reinforces this fact. This can be a clarion "call" for each adolescent. Paul's message that we are endowed with unique and varied spiritual gifts (1 Corinthians 12) is one way to reflect on this idea. Helping youth discover vocational gifts is the first step in discovering how they can best serve ("be in ministry with") others. The ongoing process of transcendence within which they seek ways of becoming and belonging is then reclaimed as a place where the church naturally stands. Confirmation grounded by such a vision is no longer viewed as a graduation, or a place of ending. It is, rather, understood as an acceptance of baptismal vows and a commissioning into ministry.

PART TWO

Resources for Confirmation

CHAPTER SEVEN

We Covenant with the Lord and One with Another

And Joshua the son of Nun was full of the spirit of
wisdom, for Moses had laid his hands upon him; so the
people of Israel obeyed him, and did as the Lord had
commanded Moses.

Deuteronomy 34:9 (RSV)

One of the most helpful skills that scouts learn is knot-tying. One knot stands out because of its usefulness; the knot that allows one to join two equal pieces of rope together—the square knot. Everyone must be familiar with rule number 1 in the rope-owner's manual: Any piece of rope one owns will invariably be too short for the task at hand. Thus, to be able to join two ropes together so that they hold fast and true is a useful skill. When joined, two pieces can accomplish goals that they could not singly.

What is it that "knots" us together into a church? What is "the tie that binds" us, as individual Christians, into what we have come to call the "church"? Though it is impossible to sum up what the church is in words, one word is emblematic for what ties us together—*covenant*. While this word is abused by our society and often used as a replacement for the word *contract*, such usage is improper. A contract is purely legal in nature, while a covenant implies a deeper form of commitment. The courts have told us that there must be three things in a legal contract: an offer, an acceptance, and a consideration. The consideration is what is exchanged. For example, you are sold a car and in exchange you give them your money. The consideration is the money exchanged for the car. There are various types of consideration, but the courts have ruled that "love," "honor," and "affection" are not considerations. This is the first spot at which contract and covenant differ. A covenant, for example means that when a ninth grader joins a Christian church, love, honor, and affection are understood as the basis for the mutual agreement by church members to be a church. It does not, of course, mean that church members always agree, but we do covenant to bear one another's burdens for the long haul.

A second difference between covenant and contract is that a covenant implies that God is an active partner in and witness to any covenant. Consider again the opening words of the Salem Church Covenant of 1629: "We covenant with the Lord and one with another to walk together in all God's ways." That is a terrific summation of what it is to be a church. There is no flowery language or ten-dollar words. Yet, these simple words speak eloquently to what it means to be a Christian. Interestingly, in that phrase "we covenant with the Lord and one with another," there is no comma to slow down our speech or our thoughts. It is implied that our covenant to care for each other and to allow ourselves to be cared for is as important as our covenant to serve God and Christ. In a strong sense, covenant implies that as Christians we are called to worship God by honoring and caring for one another and our world. We are called to recognize that love, honor, and service are the basis for our coming together to be a church which serves God. *It is into this community of ministry and response to God that we call our confirmands.*

Thus, we ask our confirmands to "bind" themselves (invoking the presence of God and Christ) to our fellowship. And just as two pieces of rope when knotted together form a longer, more useful rope, we who are joined or knotted together form a church. The following section provides the confirmation team with seven experiences to be shared with confirmands plus a retreat description that serves as a focus event for the *covenant*.

Experience 1: Heirs of the Covenant

Introduction
Youth often find it difficult to make the connection between faith and daily life. Many have trouble seeing how to be a Christian outside the church.

Purpose
This occasion is designed so that lay adults or older youth can witness to the role that faith plays in their homes, schools, and jobs.

Setting
This can take place in one of two ways. Confirmands can gather at their normal place and time, or they can go to the homes or places of employment of the persons who will be sharing their faith perspectives.

Preparation/Lead Time
Individuals should be chosen in advance. Agricultural workers, anyone in a science-related field, homemakers, judges, politicians, construction workers, and salespersons are just a few suggestions of whom might be chosen. A call or a letter should be sent asking the persons if they would be willing to share their faith. More importantly, two or more youth should be engaged to contact these individuals personally. In advance, prepare a set of questions. These questions could be determined over several meetings prior to this one, but, however formed, youth should be involved in the process.

Time
One and one-half hours.

The Experience/Process
1. Introduce the persons. Welcome them, and ask them to share with the confirmands how faith plays a role in their daily

lives. Ask each to explain their vocation and to describe a typical day. (20 minutes)

2. Encourage the ninth graders to ask the questions prepared in advance, or preferably, questions which arise from the conversation. For instance, "Do you ever think about God during the course of your day? Does being a Christian help or hinder you in your work? What does it mean to belong to this church?" (35 minutes)

3. Critically reflect upon the conversations. Discuss if/how faith plays a role in the daily lives of these church members. This is the time during which the youth should now be encouraged to discuss how faith impacts their world (whether at school, with their choir, a team, or in their home). (20 minutes)

Materials Needed
None.

So What?
This session should help the confirmand to begin to make connections between the stories of faith and the living of their lives.

Experience 2: Hanging of the Greens

Introduction
"Hanging of the Greens" is a time to learn the meanings behind some of the traditions that surround the Advent and Christmas season.

Purpose
The purpose is to bring the entire congregation together to adorn the sanctuary, listen to the traditions, and celebrate the coming season with songs, and praise and fellowship.

Setting
This activity should occur in the sanctuary, late afternoon or early evening, and include everyone, infants through senior citizens.

Preparation/Lead Time

Cast of characters and instructions for Sunday school classes need to be about three weeks ahead of the event. Poinsettias need to be ordered, greens accumulated, and costumes arranged; notes to parents, and mittens for mitten tree and refreshments.

Time

One hour for the program; 15 to 20 minutes for refreshments. Conclude with a simple service written to fit the particular church.

Materials Needed

Wreaths, Christmas tree and lights, poinsettias, nativity costumes, manger, piano, microphone system, bulletins, punch, cups, napkins, cookies, mittens.

So What?

Assigning participants from all age groups enhances the intergenerational mood: working together to decorate the sanctuary and listen to the traditions and have fellowship together. Will help to bond the many "little churches" into the united church, even if it is only for one hour. It's a start!

Experience 3: Talking History

Introduction

Seventh, eighth, and ninth graders often believe that the world revolves around them and their circle of friends. The church, however, calls us to look beyond our own familiar boundaries and into others' lives.

Purpose

This session has two purposes: (1) to promote some understanding of other generations within the church; and (2) to offer the confirmands an opportunity to record, for others' benefit, some history of their church.

Setting

Members of the church who have a story to tell about earlier days in the church's life can assemble at a scheduled time in people's homes, a pastor's office, at someone's place of employment, or somewhere else.

Preparation/Lead Time

The confirmands, a month in advance, should begin suggesting names of church members to be interviewed. You may need to make some suggestions. After deciding on a final list, these persons should be contacted (leaders had best follow up!) and scheduled to meet with the "eyewitness interview" team.

Arrangements should be made to borrow or rent a videotape camera. The confirmands should develop a set of questions designed to elicit responses about the earlier days of your church.

Time

A morning or afternoon.

The Experience/Process

1. Describe to the confirmands the goal of producing an oral video history of your church.

2. Generate potential interviewees and question list. For instance, "What is your earliest memory of this church? Toughest times? A time when this church ministered to you?"

3. Line up your interviews. Also, let the youth get comfortable with the camera before the interviews. They will at first feel silly, but after awhile their comfort level will grow.

4. Hold the interviews. Preview the tape with the class. And then, if you or they desire, hold an all-church screening some Sunday morning in the parlor.

Materials Needed

Videocamera and tapes.

So What?

The recognition that "this church has meant so much to so many" is a powerful witness to the fellowship these youth are confirming their desire to join. One does covenant with God and with each other.

Experience 4: Sanctuary Search

Introduction
A sanctuary scavenger hunt to find those symbols which have particular meaning for the Christian faith will introduce a variety of symbols to confirmands and allow them to locate these symbols on their own in the areas of your church where they are usually located. In woodwork, stained-glass windows, altars, and artwork, the meanings of our faith may come to life and be made more real for the young people.

Purpose
As opposed to straight teaching and testing, the scavenger search provides the confirmands with a different kind of experience, one of finding the symbols for themselves and trying to detect the symbolic meanings on their own. In a fun and active way, the kids are turned loose on the church, as Christian anthropologists and historians, in order to decipher the meanings to our symbols of faith. By the end of the session, each youth should be able to identify and understand a variety of symbols.

Setting
The introduction should take place wherever you usually meet with the confirmands. From there confirmands are released into the areas of the church that contain the sought-after symbols. The sanctuary is usually the area that is most replete with symbols. This experience may be done in an hour-long session and should take place during the daylight hours in order to be able to see the art in stained-glass windows. This may be done in teams, pairs, or as individuals, as long as everyone participates.

Preparation/Lead Time
Time is needed for the leadership to prepare the scavenger hunt sheet. It is important that this sheet be custom-made so it con-

forms to the particular symbols found in your church. For example, if there is not a Chi/Rho present in your sanctuary, no one will be able to find one!

Allow time for research and/or study on the part of the leadership. Find a book on Christian symbols, and make sure you are familiar with the traditional meanings of these symbols.[1] Know as many as you can, as the youth may ask questions about symbols which are not found in your sanctuary. Be prepared for anything.

Possible symbols include, but are not limited to: the lighted lamp; chi/rho, alpha/omega; Lamb of God; open Bible; hand of God; two tablets (Ten Commandments); the ship; fleur-de-lis; descending dove; the fish ("ichthus"); "IHS"; "INRI"; the Good Shepherd; the cross; chalice, loaf/grapes/wheat; the crown; butterfly; quatrefoil; three interlocking circles; lighted candle; water; disciples' symbols (book, purse, lion, keys, etc.); cloud (nimbus); the rainbow; touching fingers; halos; cherub/angels; colors of the church year; and so on.

A knowledge of these symbols will also be helpful for the discussion at the end of the session.

Time

About one hour.

The Experience/Process

1. As the session begins, welcome the confirmands as if they are esteemed Christian historians. Refer to them as "Doctor" or "Professor." Then introduce the concept of the use of symbolism in our faith. Why do we use symbols? What are some recognizable symbols in modern society? (5 minutes)

2. Distribute the scavenger hunt sheets. Explain the task at hand. They are to consider themselves Christian historians and find the symbols on the sheet. As the symbols are found, each youth is to make an educated guess as to the meaning of each symbol. Be sure to deal with any other ground rules here (where to go, where not to go, etc.) and with any questions they may have. (2–3 minutes)

3. Send the confirmands forth on their task of filling out the

sheet. Be available to help out with questions or hints during the experience. (20–25 minutes)

4. Reconvene and discuss. Go over the sheet and ask what answers they came up with for each new discovery. At this point, ask what the traditional meanings of the symbols are and how we interpret them in the light of faith. (remaining time)

5. Close with a prayer of thanksgiving, or recite together the Apostle's Creed (or another historical creed). This seeks to make yet another connection to our faithful ancestors.

Materials Needed
Scavenger search sheets, pencils or pens.

So What?
Two results are hoped for here. First, the confirmands may gain new insights into the symbols of Christianity. Our faith is more than a religion or a set of words. We also express faith through art, symbolism, and actions. Early Christians lived in a dangerous time, so they had to use symbolic representations to be safe from those who persecuted them. This may evolve into a discussion of how Christians are persecuted around the globe today, or what it is like to be a faithful person in a secular society.

The second result is that the church building may now come alive for the youth in ways they had not experienced before. Worship is sometimes seen as a boring experience in a sanctuary filled with adults, long sermons, and classical music. If the youth are distracted during worship, they may look at the symbols in the sanctuary in a new light and consider their faith in relation to them.

Experience 5: World's Greatest Chain Letter

Introduction
The laying on of hands should be a powerful experience for the confirmand. It is an ancient and awe-filled tradition that symbolizes the power of the Holy Spirit at work in our world.

Purpose

This experience will aid the confirmands in gaining a deeper understanding of the Rite of Confirmation and specifically the act of the laying on of hands.

Setting

This should be a regular meeting, but one that is close to the Rite of Confirmation. Older youth, sponsors, the members of the congregation, and ordained clergy may participate.

Preparation/Lead Time

Ask an ordained pastor to meet with those youth who are ready to experience the Rite of Confirmation. This person should take some time to reflect on the process of ordination and the laying on of hands experienced at that moment. If your tradition has laying on of hands for deacons, elders, commissioned lay workers, fraternal workers, or others, invite one or two of them to share these personal reflections.

Time

One hour.

The Experience/Process

1. Introduce the session by explaining the tradition of the laying on of hands. A good resource in this area is *The Oxford Dictionary of the Christian Church.*[2] A good analogy to explain the laying on of hands is the chain letter. The laying on of hands is an ancient tradition during which the church invokes the Holy Spirit to be bestowed upon those who confirm baptismal vows. The gesture in which ordained place hands upon the confirmand symbolizes the presence and communication of the Spirit. For most Protestant traditions, this is the sacramental sign of confirmation. (5 minutes)

2. Ask the confirmands to look up several Bible passages which deal with this act, for example, Acts 8:15-17, 8:19, 6:1-6, and Mark 10:16. Discuss these passages and their connection with this group's upcoming Rite of Confirmation. (20 minutes)

3. Share with the class that an unbroken chain of Christians has been engaged in passing on the Spirit of Christ for centuries.

During this process actually place your hands on the heads of several persons. Reflect with them on the just-shared memories of the laying on of hands. If you are reflecting on your own ordination, share the name of who confirmed you, and if you know it, the name of who confirmed that person. Most youth I have met are awed by the power of the "world's greatest chain letter."

4. Guide the class, using newsprint or blackboard, into a discussion to help the confirmand define what is meant by the invocation of "spirit." Is it this spirit that is with you in your compassion to care for others? Is it the feeling you get when singing a song around a campfire on retreat? What spirit can we claim as being present with us now? (15 minutes)

5. Conclude with an open prayer which includes space for the confirmands to respond to God in prayer about the Holy Spirit and the laying on of hands.

Materials Needed

None.

So What?

The Rite of Confirmation and the laying on of hands is, or can be, filled with awe and mystery. This session is a way intentionally to open the confirmands' eyes to the tradition and power of this activity.

Focus Event on Covenant: Community

Introduction

A retreat offers a condensed block of time away from the known routine in which people become embedded. A Friday after-school departure (with sack "suppers" for travel) to a long-in-advance reserved retreat center for a weekend retreat can become, with foresight, a high spot in a confirmation program.

Purpose

This retreat is structured with enough of a caring, low-risk framework to provide those who have never gone on a retreat before with some helpful ways to build a group. At the same time, the theological/spiritual perspective is embodied as an integral part of what goes on.

Setting

Because retreats are popular, a retreat center should be booked well in advance. *Note:* School calendars present important dates on which no retreat should occur. Also consider other important yearly events that impact your context.

Retreat centers sometimes provide options regarding food; i.e., it will cost more if others cook your food, but if your group is large, the time saved may be of importance. You may decide to do a retreat on private property: someone's cottage by the lake, or another church in a nearby town. Distance, cost, and the size of your group are factors impacting retreat decisions. In addition, if you go to a ski lodge in winter, for example, the setting offers (and perhaps imposes) the agenda. This retreat is designed for a group that wants to get to know each other better within an intentional Christian framework; it is not a design that fits a ski weekend.

Preparation/Lead Time

Confirmands should know a long time in advance about the retreat. Letters (including the purpose of the retreat, where it is, cost, emergency phone, permission slip, doctor's release form, etc.) should be sent to parents, and a date set for sign-up and for payment of fees. Some churches subsidize such events; others run bake sales to defray costs, but an issue to be dealt with long in advance has to do with whether advisors (older youth and/or adults) will be asked to pay, and who will be allowed to drive. Medical insurance on the retreat, driver coverage, and legal liability issues need to be considered. Some of the items called for in this retreat design (Scavenger hunt instructions, a "crankie," etc.) will also need to be prepared in advance of the event.

The Experience Process

The retreat begins as people wander into the church near departure time. People will need to be helped in the loading of cars and the detail work (all payments, permissions, sleeping bags, equipment, etc., on board?). I still like to use Dr. Sidney Simon's I.A.L.A.C. sign—a three-by-five-inch card which reads I.A.L.A.C. with a yarn loop for wearing around a neck—that is hung on every person before leaving. Give no answer to what I.A.L.A.C. stands for except that, "We'll find out [Friday] night."[3]

Activity 1

After the group has settled into the retreat center, noted the camp rules, and taken a quick hike to acclimate, reconvene in a group for Activity 1. Explain that people often wear masks to hide how they really feel. If possible, have several masks (i.e., costume, Halloween) to play with as you suggest the idea that we often present one image to the world but sense inside that we are very different.

Pass out two three-by-five-inch cards. Assure completely confidentiality in that no names are to be written on any card. On one card encourage everyone to draw (stick figures) on one side how someone they know looks on the outside; on the other side have them draw (stick figures) how someone they know looks like on the inside. With the second card, have them draw on one side how they sense *they* look on the outside, and on the reverse side how they look on the inside.

Collect all the cards; shuffle them and pass out one card per person. (No one can receive his or her own card.)

Read, tell, or present the story of Lazarus (John 11:1, 3:17–19, 32–35, 38–41, and 43–44). A "crankie" might be used. A simple crankie is a large roll of white paper wound tightly around a broomstick, ready to be rolled, or "cranked," onto another broomstick. The rolled paper is a cartoonlike characterization of the story which will be told as the paper is cranked from broomstick to broomstick. A simple broomstick crankie with no frame is shown in figure 1. In the crankie there are no neat cartoon boxes; each scene fades into the next, and the more amateurish the stick figures, the better people respond. Use color for feelings, and design the crankie with the size of your audience in mind.

Ask for reflection on the card each person is holding. How

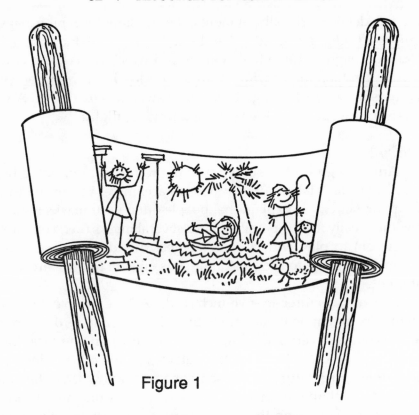

Figure 1

alive/how bound is this person? Are they alive/bound/in-between regarding their relationships? Emotions? Thoughts? If Jesus knew this person, what would he say?

Do the same with the rest of the cards.

Conclude with retelling the Lazarus story.

Activity 2

The "Paper Bag-not-ready-for-prime-time" theater will take about 45 minutes to get ready. If you have a minimum of ten people (including advisors), divide in half and provide both groups with paper bags filled with an assortment of props (masks, wigs, clothes, plastic gun, and whatever you have found). Every prop must be used and every person must be involved in presentation of a skit. (You might give each group three parables from which they can choose one story line to update using the props.)

View the skits. Eat popcorn.

Activity 3

If you know the retreat center, an outdoor hike is in order. If it is raining, a film appropriate to the topic might be shown, but a change of pace is desired to slow down the group, aiming at a late-night telling of the I.A.L.A.C. ("I am lovable and capable") story. Around midnight, announce that everyone could get ready for bed and then assemble in one area. Invite them to bring sleeping bags. Have one to three candles as the only light, and have one person ready to tell the I.A.L.A.C. story.

Dr. Sidney Simon in *I Am Lovable and Capable* tells the story about Randy, a ninth grader who gets up early in the morning wearing his I.A.L.A.C. sign. Randy suffers many mishaps during the day, ranging from being attacked by some gang members and having to turn in sloppy homework to not having anyone at home when he arrives after school and not being able to call up a potential girlfriend because of low self-image. At each point, Randy loses a piece of his I.A.L.A.C. sign. But the next day he gets up with a new sign around his neck.

This story clicks with most adolescents. Having read the story, discuss it and how I.A.L.A.C. impacts this retreat and a church community, share prayer, and then go to bed—lights out in one hour.

Activity 4

Community can become cozy within four walls. Eventually this group must move out or wither and die. Simulation games mirror reality by placing people into situations with a payoff. Frequently the simulation idea slides away as the strains of reality occur *now*. Some aspects of community are tested. Most participants come away strengthened.

1. This simulation is an early morning interdependency/communication game, but it is much more than a game. It can provide the deep experience of being together and working together in a simulated situation of need. It can be used with groups large or small.

2. Divide the larger group into smaller groups. Put the directions for each group into an envelope. Pass slips to each person in the group. The slips here reflect a group of ten participants.

Four slips say: "You cannot speak for the rest of the game. You can see but you cannot speak. From this point on you may not talk."

Four slips say: "You cannot see for the rest of the game. You can speak but you cannot see. From this point on you cannot see." (Provide blindfolds for the "blind.")

Two slips say: "You are an observer, and your task is to follow the group. Do not assist the group in any way. Your task is to observe. There is one exception. If members of the group get into a situation that is potentially dangerous, intervene so that no one is hurt. Things to watch for: How did your group work together? How was leadership dealt with? How did the group organize itself? How did the group deal with the problem of communication? Was there trust or mistrust in the group?"

3. In an envelope given to each group, Directive no. 1 is included. "Your group is to proceed to [state location]. Look for the next directive at that place."

Directive no. 2: "You have been in a car wreck. Two members of your group have broken legs and must be carried, one observer has been blinded. Your group is to proceed to [location]. Look for the next directive in that place."

Directive no. 3: "You have been mugged. Two more in the group have been blinded, one more has a broken leg. Proceed to [location]."

4. With minimum instructions, each group discovers that they need to help one another, organize themselves to follow the directives, and find ways to communicate with one another. The directives can move the groups up and down stairs, over not-too-difficult walls and barriers, and outside for distances of not more than five hundred to one thousand feet. The game could be played over a period of time, including a meal. This makes the payoff quite real. The final directive should bring the groups back to the point of origin.

5. Debriefing of the events and the feelings associated with the events is a necessary part of the game. Check out what happened. See if parallels can be drawn to what "community" is all about.

Ask: "In what way was this like school, military, church, or our group? Was it realistic? Did it clarify anything for you?" The observers should be asked to comment. Questions of organization, leadership, communication, being dependent, and helping others should be discussed. Use as much time as is needed.

Activity 5

Meals can be times for song, prayer, or reflection on a poster that is taped onto a wall. Youth can be mentored into sharing these moments of thanks.

Activity 6

After lunch, divide the group in half, put one set of names in a hat and let the other set draw partners. Gather everyone in a single room to sit with their partner.

The leader notes that everyone in the room has gifts from God, and that the partners will work through a series of timed exercises in anticipation or discovering these gifts. (The following exercise was timed, with numbers 1 through 4 distributed as needed on separate sheets of paper prepared in advance.)

Distribute and read sheet no. 1.

This exercise is to help you find out what "gifts" your partner has. Everyone is different. Some people enjoy dancing; other people like to swim. Some have a talent for writing or singing; others enjoy being with people. Some people are warm and friendly and make a group very comfortable. Others bubble and seem to spread fun and smiles wherever they go. Others are quiet, yet when they speak seem to have sensed just what is going on.

Immediately distribute sheet no. 2:

You have approximately ten minutes to complete this sheet. What would you do if you have "a perfect day" all to yourself? Describe this day. Who would be with you? Where would you be? What would you experience?

Time the completion of sheet no. 2, encouraging discussion. Partners should decide who will go first in sharing the "perfect day," then ask questions, pursue each idea, and get to "know" each other. Once completed, move to sheet no. 3.

Complete these sentences:
Something I do well is _____ .
The way I feel when I am doing this is _____ .
This requires me to have the ability to _____ .
When I am with others doing this I feel _____ .

Time the completion of sheet No. 3 and the sharing of that accompanies it, and then distribute sheet no. 4.

In my room at home are several important things that define who I am. If my house burned down, I'd want to save _____ . The reason this is important to me and I'd want to save it is that _____ .

The leader encourages completion of and discussion of sheet no. 4. When finished, each participant is handed a fifth sheet:

Isolate one word that begins to sum up the uniqueness and the gifts of the person who has been sharing with you. Use this worksheet to write a cinquain about this person.

The gift is this, in one word:
These two words describe the gift:
Here is a short sentence about the gift:
These two adverbs (end in "-ly") also describe the gift:
One final word, in summary:

With sheets 1 through 4 completed, each person can choose a piece of bright construction paper, fold it like a card, enclose the cinquain as a poem, address the card to the partner, sign it, and add a logo or trademark. An example:

To Rich:
Compassionate, Caring, Sympathetic
You enjoy helping other people!
Understanding, friendly, loving!
[signed] Ellen

Cards can be shared or saved ("mailed") for an evening common worship celebration.

Activity 7

Time should be set aside to read, hike, exercise, sing, take showers, play games.

Activity 8

In the evening, as it grows dark, read the Jerusalem Bible's version of the Beatitudes:

> *How happy are the poor in spirit:*
> *theirs is the [Dominion] of Heaven.*
> *How happy the gentle:*
> *they shall have the earth for their heritage.*
> *Happy those who mourn:*
> *they shall be comforted.*
> *Happy those who hunger and thirst for what is right:*
> *they shall be satisfied.*
> *Happy those who show mercy:*
> *they shall have mercy shown them.*
> *Happy the pure in heart:*
> *they shall see God.*
> *Happy the peacemakers:*
> *they shall be called sons of God.*
> *Happy those who are persecuted in the cause of right:*
> *theirs is the [Dominion] of Heaven.*
>
> *Matthew 5 (Jerusalem Bible)*

Then either divide into small groups, or use "squirms" on the convened whole group. "Squirms" are a handful of questions dealing with the Beatitudes folded into a small can. Each person pulls a slip of paper from the can and responds, i.e., "squirms." The group then joins the discussion. Examples of "squirms":

> *"If you want to get ahead in life you have to step on a few people." Do you agree? Disagree? Why, or why not?*
>
> *The "Dominion of Heaven": Some people say it is a place— with gold floors and hundreds of angels floating around. Others say it is a relationship of God to us and we with one another, insisted on by Jesus as available right now, not in the future. What do you believe the "Dominion of Heaven" is? If you think it is a place, how*

do you get there? If you think it is a relationship, *how does this affect your life?*

What does "happy" mean to you? The Beatitudes all start with the word happy, *or in some old translations the word* blessed *is used. Give four sentences starting with "Happy is _____ ," or "Happy are _____ ," or "Blessed are _____ ."*

Can you name two people who have been or are being "persecuted in the cause of right"? Why were they not welcomed with love and kindness?

Are Christians being persecuted today? Is being a Christian something different from being a human involved "in the cause of right"? The Beatitudes bless *the person doing* right and avoids *those who* label themselves *as doing right. Why?*

"Peace." What is peace? Are you a peace-maker? If you are not a peacemaker, does this automatically mean you are a war monger? Why or why not?

Christ was gentle, yet strong. He loved little children, but drove the money-changers from the "temple." Is this inconsistent? How do you picture Jesus? As a weak sissy, or a strong man? What did he look like in your mind? How can a man be gentle, yet strong?

Alan was arrested for demonstrating at a peace rally. He had broken the law by marching in the street. There was no violence, but Alan spent the night in jail. Is Alan a peacemaker? Why, or why not?

Fill in the sentences: I am a peacemaker because I _____ . I am not a peacemaker because I _____ .

The line goes, "Happy are those who hunger and thirst for what is right, for they shall be satisfied." What is "right"? What is "satisfaction"? Using your definitions for "right" and "satisfaction," are you involved in doing "right"? Are you "satisfied" with your life?

Activity 9

Later in the evening gather folk for worship. Center the worship around communion. Use candles, appropriate readings, opportunities to discuss joys and concerns, and a structured period of sharing the dyad cinquain cards. The *individual* gets to keep the card.

Activity 10

Sunday morning's activity centers around food. Here we experience worship, community, trust, togetherness, and joy in a unique way.

1. Furnish meat, carrots, cauliflower, tomatoes, sardines, chocolate chips.

2. Gather everyone in a room away from the dining area. There, talk about your own feelings concerning the retreat. Mention specific good things that happened. Refer to Christ's ideas of love, and how it's tough, not a once-and-for-all mountaintop experience, but a daily living-out-love experience.

3. Then give directions for your final meal: (a) the meal will be nonverbal; that is, no talking; (b) you cannot feed yourself; that is, you can only feed others; (c) you may refuse to accept food offered.

4. Go to the meal. The wilder the food, the better. And don't have chairs; standing up and moving around is better. Furnish no forks; instead, use toothpicks and fingers.

5. Near the end, two people could circulate with a large loaf of bread and chalice of wine. The meaning of the gift was never better expressed.

Activity 11

Returning home: things have happened on this retreat. It's been a very heavy time. Some moments of reflection are in order after the facilities are cleaned and everyone is packed. Ask for comments. Check the I.A.L.A.C.'s. Thank the staff.

Instruct participants to do the following: Gather in a circle. Look around at the people. For several moments just check who's been here; say "hi" with your eyes. Now close your eyes—think about the weekend—I.A.L.A.C., the simulation game, the communion, the softball game, the nonverbal meal. Now think about going home, being tired, meeting families, sleeping, school the next day. Think about how you feel: Happy? Sad? Tired? Think, too, of the people you know just a bit better and of the community discovered in an old house off in the woods.

Ask everyone to open their eyes; share now the familiar benediction, "May the Lord watch _____ ," or the song "Shalom."

Activity 12

A safe journey home, and a letter to all parents later that week detailing what happened on retreat. Common worship in the church should have a moment, later on, to hear a confirmand report on the retreat.

CHAPTER EIGHT

Experiencing the Tradition

In Jesus, God has said *Yes* and *Amen* to it all, and that
Yes and *Amen* is the firm ground on which we stand.

Dietrich Bonhoeffer
Letters and Papers from Prison

Young persons about to be confirmed are engaged in the public affirmation of either the vows taken in baptism or, if unbaptized,
their personal decision to walk with God and their church on a
faith journey. Certainly this does not occur in a vacuum; they have
already taken numerous steps along this journey. These steps may
be compared to the stages a young child goes through when learning to draw.

First a young child scribbles, moving the crayon *randomly* every which way. There is no plan or premeditated idea to the child's
actions or movements. Then a second stage emerges as the child
begins to exert some *control* over the crayon. Instead of random
motion, the child's movements become more controlled and more
deliberate. For instance, the child now draws lines and circles, cop-
ied from the environment. But, as children grow, they enter the
stage in which deliberate movements with a crayon are used to
symbolize an idea. It is at this naming stage that a child intentionally connects meaning to the act of drawing. Five lines and a circle
no longer are just five lines and a circle. Now, these five lines are
connected and topped by a circle to create a "human being"—a
stick figure.

As the spiritual journey central to confirmation moves into
a deeper understanding of God's role in one's life, confirmands
parallel these steps of scribble, control, and naming. The first
stage in the faith journey is akin to scribbling, that is, very similar

to a child's random movement in its random play and explosive exuberance.

As the pilgrimage continues, a confirmand's movements become much more deliberate. Much of what we recognize as church school education is an attempt to influence and help to meet this stage. The resources of faith are acquired as tools. For example, acting out the parable of the good Samaritan means that someone reads from a script, follows the teacher's directions, and reenacts the biblical parable. In the family or at church children learn to bow their heads and fold their hands while praying, even though they may not necessarily know why; they do it because they see important others doing it. And when children share in communion they eat the piece of bread and press the cup to their lips in imitation of those around them. By imitating others, one learns how to participate in the community, a most important lesson.

The third and final state, naming, is the most demanding of the three. It is here that the confirmand must ask, "What do such deliberate movements symbolize for me?" Confirmation seeks critical reflection at this point, and it is because of this need that we believe confirmation should *not* occur before ninth grade. Here those five lines topped by a circle are not just a stick figure, but represent in a symbolic, abstract, reflective way, the meaning assigned to God. Here one begins to see the good Samaritan not as "the funny kid in your Sunday school class with a strange-looking robe on," but as "someone who helps in a time of crisis." In the naming stage of faith, one begins to see God's presence in the face of a Samaritan, a place where we would least have expected it.

Confirmands are asked to hear, critically reflect on, and ultimately affirm those stories, movements, and rituals that symbolize our faith in God's work in history and in our lives. While these acts of the Christian tradition can be acquired by rote, authentically naming their significance for each individual is very tough to do. It requires a covenantal setting and a personal decision to seek the truth. Confirmation is therefore a unique opportunity *to critically assess and name* communal and personal meaning. Here is where the faith story and vision intersect with life. All the rich resources of what we call the Christian tradition are involved in such naming. While such resources have perhaps remained hidden, with little or no impact regarding the faithful life of the confirmands, we believe that opportunities for critical reflection emerging from experiential encounters with these traditions are essential to the faithful life of an adolescent in this age. We hope that the following experiences begin to move the confirmands into the naming stage of their faith journeys.

Experience 6A: Who Is Jesus?

Introduction

The question, "Who are you?" has been asked continuously since Jesus Christ walked the earth. Even Jesus asked his disciples, "Who do people say that I am?" (Mark 8:27). Prophet, miracle worker, teacher, and/or personal Savior are among the variety of images of Jesus that exist in the Scriptures. They all may answer the question, "Who is Jesus?"

Purpose

This activity will familiarize the confirmands with the myriad images of Jesus that comprise the "Risen One."

Setting

The gathered community of faith should assemble at the regular meeting time in any part of the church where you have access to a television and video-cassette player (for the first session).

Preparation/Lead Time

Several weeks in advance, call or write Paulist Productions and order the film, *Ecce Homo.*[1]

Time

One hour.

The Experience/Process

1. Introduce to the group your plan to study the question, "Who is Jesus?" for the next two sessions. Solicit from them their images of who Jesus was/is. Their responses will depend on their

level of development and familiarity with the Bible. (10 minutes)

2. Explain the idea that in the days when most persons were illiterate, art was one of the ways of spreading the Word to the people. Stained glass, icons, music, and frescoes, for example, were all channels through which the people saw or heard the stories of Jesus. The confirmands are about to see and hear the story themselves. Show the movie. (30 minutes)

3. Following the movie, clarify any questions or confusions anyone might have about the story. Use the questions as discussion starters to elicit different responses to the movie. Questions are provided with the movie and, in general, are helpful. (15 minutes)

4. Ask that in the coming week, the confirmands try to identify one image of Jesus found in their world, whether it be school, home, television, etc.

Materials Needed

Television and video-cassette player or 16mm projector (film available in both), film (see address in note 1), flip chart, and pen.

So What?

In this session the confirmand will be exposed to a broad look at the life of Jesus in scripture and art. The film is an excellent beginning for a deeper examination of the question, "Who is Jesus?"

Experience 6B: Who Is Jesus?

Preparation/Lead Time

The leader should read the Bible verses listed below before the confirmands assemble a second time.

Time

One and one-half hours.

The Experience/Process

1. Open this second session by recapping the confirmands' thoughts from the movie *Ecce Homo*. Then ask one youth to look up

Mark 8:27-30 and read the passage aloud. Have several persons assigned to the various voices reread the passage. Ask the class, "Who do *you* say that Jesus is?" Write down their responses. (10 minutes)

2. Divide the class into quarters and give each group the appropriate Bible verses which describe different images of Jesus. Have magazines available and ask each group to read their verses, decide what image they have, and create a collage of that image (for instance, for the prophet image, one girl cut out a picture of a mouse pulling an elephant). Have each group present their "painting" of Jesus.

Appropriate verses are as follows: *Jesus as Prophet*—Matthew 5:17-20, 24:1-14; Luke 6:27-31. You may need to define *prophet* (in the biblical sense for the group. Ask them to identify modern prophets (Martin Luther King, Gandhi, etc.) or social critics (newspaper columnist Mike Royko, etc.) *Jesus as Teacher*—Any of the parables and/or the Beatitudes could be used here. *Jesus and Healer/Miracle Worker*—Mark 4:39, 3:1-6, 3:7-12. *Jesus as Savior/Child of God*—Luke 17:20-21; John 3:31, 36-38. (30 minutes)

Materials Needed
Bibles, scissors, magazines, glue, cardboard.

So What?
To begin to profess one's own faith one must have a scriptural understanding of "who Jesus is." This session is a good framework on which to build the confirmation program.

Experience 7: Chalcedon

Introduction
Questions about Jesus have been with Christians for centuries. For example, in 431 C.E., Christians gathered for the Council of Chalcedon with the hope of answering the question, "Is Jesus human or divine?"

Purpose

This simulation hopes to impact the confirmands as they think about their own beliefs concerning the humanity/divinity of Jesus Christ. Also, this will help familiarize confirmands with the initial process by which humans declared a certain collection of writings (the Bible) as the "standard" by which all other such writings were to be judged.

Setting

Two tables should be set up facing each other, along with a "bishop's chair" placed at the head of the room. This should be a confirmation community meeting, with all participating. An adult or youth leader should play the role of moderator (explained below).

Preparation/Lead Time

A brief history of the Council of Chalcedon should be reviewed.[2] The leader should have prepared printed slips of Bible verses which are "proofs" of Jesus' humanity or divinity. A few passages should reflect both sides so as to promote discussion, for example, regarding Jesus' *humanity:* Hebrews 5:7, John 19:26-27, 19:28-30, Matthew 27:39-42, 27:46; on Jesus' *divinity:* Hebrews 1:1, Luke 20:26-29, Matthew 27:39-42. There are, of course, many more readings that emphasize both understandings.

Time

At least one hour.

The Experience/Process

1. Introduce the background of the council to the group and tell them that you are hoping that they can come to an answer about the human/divine question. Choose a "bishop" (an older youth or adult leader) to moderate the debate. (5 minutes)

2. Split the group in half by birthdays (January-June birthdays will defend Jesus as human; July-December birthdays will defend Jesus' divinity), and have each group look up the appropriate defenses of their position. (10 minutes)

3. Have the bishop convene the council and open the debate

with the question: "So, is Jesus human or divine? We must come to an answer to this perplexing question."

4. Inform each person to prepare to vote on the question: Is Jesus human? divine? human *and* divine? Instruct them to vote based on their personal beliefs and not necessarily on which side they were for the debate. Ask those who are willing to cast their vote and to share their reasons. (10 minutes)

5. Conclude by informing the class that the Council of Chalcedon voted that Jesus was *both* human and divine, and that we, as Christians, continue to affirm this position. Such a discussion may continue beyond the single hour allotted.

Materials Needed
Slips of paper with Bible verses.

So What?
This simulation will assist the confirmand in beginning to understand that our faith is connected to certain positions developed sixteen hundred years ago. The mystery of God and questions about Jesus, however, are timeless.

Experience 8: Encountering Parables

Introduction
Research tells us that Jesus took everyday experiences of the people around him and turned them into the foundations of his parables. As a result, they deeply touched the lives of the listeners. Times have changed radically since then. We have lost touch with the commonness of the parables, and they have lost much of their power in hearing. Yet we can relive those times by attending to the parables and translating them into contemporary form through our imagination.

Purpose
This activity is designed to help the confirmands relive the stories of Jesus in ways that will both increase their knowledge of scripture and integrate their learning into daily living.

Setting

This experience can be done almost anywhere, as long as the surroundings don't upstage the experience. If you have an interactive environment that will draw attention to itself, e.g., outdoors with rain or dogs, loud noises, lots of movement, etc., then it would be better to move to a less interactive space. It is helpful for the group to be rested or at least for the exercise to be done at a time when the community has some energy and enthusiasm reserves. It is also helpful for the group to have had a chance to get to know each other beforehand.

Preparation/Lead Time

Familiarize yourself with the tradition of Jesus' use of parables in the Bible. Find and make a few copies of a list of the parables. Familiarize yourself enough with at least one parable and its background that you could tell it in your own words. Find a new ice-breaker or two that everyone can learn together. Silly ones are helpful here.

Time

75–90 minutes.

The Experience/Process

1. Since everyone knows each other, use ice-breakers not as get-acquainted games, but to help remove the inhibitions that we all bring to a new experience. Everyone needs a safe place to try on new things and new selves. (10–15 minutes)

2. As an introduction, share with the youth your understanding of how Jesus used parables and their link with everyday experiences. (5 minutes)

3. Divide the group into subgroups of four to six. You know your group best. Sometimes self-selection is counter-productive, and you will spend more time on group process than on the experience at hand. Random selection is sometimes a good alternative. (2–3 minutes)

4. Have each group select and read a parable, first silently and then aloud. Have them brainstorm about what they think the ev-

eryday experience might have been like. Then have them do some background reading on the parable. It is ideal to have each participant read a different commentary and then share what was learned. (15 minutes)

5. Have the youth create a short skit based on the scripture and its background. It is important to give a good deal of freedom here with a number of suggestions, such as the following: one person reading the scripture and another miming it out; all doing an improvisation on what they found the common experience was like then; or all doing an improvisation in modern-day life from what they found the common experience was like then. (15 minutes)

6. Have each group perform for the others. Play it up, introduce each group, encourage applause, etc. (3–5 minutes)

7. As a whole group if less than fifteen youth, or by pairing play groups if you have a large group, give each youth a chance to share what she or he has learned. Help them to focus on the similarities and differences between then and now, and how their learning changed when they put what they learned into the action of an improvisation. Help them to generalize this experience to their everyday lives. (10 minutes)

Materials Needed

A list of the parables of Jesus, one for every four youth; Bibles, at least one for every two youth is helpful; Bible commentaries, at least one for every four youth; more if possible (your pastor may help here if you want some diversity in your commentaries); paper and pencils for notes.

So What?

It is commonly said that to understand someone you must first "walk a mile in their moccasins." Merely thinking about who they were would not do. In the same way this experience will help the participants understand more fully the intentions of Jesus in his use of the parables. He came to transform the world in practice, not just in theory. We endeavor to do the same thing with the young people with whom we work. Just as we as leaders can be changed in the process, with this exercise we open the door for the spirit to work through the imaginations of the young people, bringing them to a fuller understanding.

Experience 9: Singing the Lord's Song

Introduction
The Word has been shared in the form of music for centuries. It is, of course, one of the most powerful media for touching a person's soul.

Purpose
This experience will familiarize the youth with the great, but ever-changing, tradition of Christian music.

Setting
The choir room, or any place where taped music can be played.

Preparation/Lead Time
Arrange with the music/choir director to borrow from your local library a taped selection of music from different eras. One director we know begins with Gregorian chants, moves into antiphonal singing, the Reformation period, and so on, up to modern anthems and Christian rock.

Time
One hour.

The Experience/Process
1. Have a person familiar with this tradition make a presentation. Also, have the presenter explain the hymnal and its history.
2. If possible, gather the group in the sanctuary for a chance to sit at the piano or organ. Explain how it works, where it came from, and of course, play it for the group, encouraging them to sing.
3. After the presentation, confirmands remain in the sanctuary

and look for other ways to "tell the story." Point out symbols, stained glass, and so on.

Materials Needed
Recorded music and a player.

So What?
This session helps the confirmands recognize that the Word may be shared in many ways. Music is one of the media through which we worship God and witness to the role God plays in our lives.

Experience 10: Luther and the Reformation

Introduction
Martin Luther was, of course, the central figure of the Protestant Reformation. A basic understanding of who he was is central for an understanding of Protestantism today.

Purpose
This activity will familiarize the confirmands with the story of Luther's life and the basic issues of the Protestant Reformation.

Setting
Your regular classroom.

Preparation/Lead Time
The leader should order well in advance the film, *Where Luther Walked*, available from Mass Media.[3]

Time
One hour.

The Experience/Process
1. Introduce Luther and the basic tenets of the Reformation. Most encyclopedias will have a brief but good summary.
2. Show the film. Be prepared to stop the film at points where

the community may seem confused. Respond to any questions and continue. (40 minutes)

3. Ask the community to reconstruct Luther's life and to respond to scenes in the film which were memorable.

Materials Needed
VCR/TV or 16mm film projector.

So What?
Luther was an extraordinary man who altered the political and religious landscapes of Europe and western culture. Thus, some basic knowledge of who he was and what he did is an essential resource for a mature faith.

Focus Event on Tradition: Ten from the Top

Introduction
Adults who serve as mentors in the confirmation process or youth who serve as a peer staff may be challenged along with the confirmands as they engage in these two sessions which are centered upon the Ten Commandments.[4] Each commandment summed up an ethical position to be taken when faced with difficult and often seductive alternatives. Jesus condensed the thrust of the Ten Commandments into the single phrase: "Love God and your neighbor as yourself." The following exercise provides a variety of difficult contextual issues into which specific "commandments" are introduced. The resultant choices and interpretations made by the mentors and confirmands should provoke thoughtful reflection on how we are called to live.

Purpose
By providing common experiences open to interpretation by both youth and adults, these exercises engage participants in a shared common task; they become peers focused on what could/should happen in a given context. The resultant action and con-

versation will encourage not only reflection on the commandments but a stronger mentoring relationship within the confirmation process.

Setting

If the commandments are divided, two sequential gatherings (on a weeknight or Sunday afternoon) would be one possibility for a church setting or a mentor's home. With additional material an overnight mini-retreat might be envisioned in a cottage, church, or retreat center.

Preparation/Lead Time

Extensive preparation is called for, in that each commandment requires props and a written set of directions.

The Experience/Process

While the process can be done with large confirmation groups, it is based upon individual response. Commandments 1 through 6 assume one respondent, 7 and 8 assume three participants, 9 and 10 assume three or more.

Steps A, B, and C are used for each commandment studied. Step D may be used at the end of one program, at the end of each program, or at the end of the third and final program only.

Set a large box in the middle of the group. Inside this box are three or four smaller boxes (depending on which program design you are using) or ten smaller boxes if you are doing all in one long program, each with an envelope glued to the lid (to be opened before the box is opened) and an envelope glued to the bottom (to be opened after the box has been opened).

Step A

Anyone willing to draw a small box from the large box is initially to read the lid envelope and then to carry out its instructions. Then the person does the same with the bottom envelope. (Note: The boxes are numbered by number of commandment but do not have to be taken in numerical order during each program.)

Step B

The leader/enabler has a "position statement" for each box, which is to be used immediately after the box process. Place three pieces of cardboard on the floor before the position statement is read. The first piece reads, "For Sure." The second reads, "Maybe/Maybe Not." The third reads, "No Way." Read the statement:

> Example: *"The commandment, 'You shall have no other gods before me,' means that anyone who owns a Rolls Royce is not honoring God."*

After the statement is read, each participant positions himself/herself on one of the three available cardboard signs. Then encourage discussion. See whether anyone wants to reposition after discussion.

To sharpen the discussion, sometimes get the folks who are standing at one of the positions to work up an argument for why everyone in the room should be standing where they are standing. Also, from time to time, after the participants have a feel for the Position Statement, divide the group into small groups to write their own statements for the whole group to use.

Step C

Ask everyone to respond to some of the following comments: "The most important thing I learned in this study was _____ ." "Something I had never thought of before is _____ ." "What I'll be most likely to remember from this study is _____ ."

Step D

Ask participants to rank the commandments from number 1 through whatever number was studied, with number 1 as "the most helpful for me/us as youth today," number 2 as "the next most helpful," and so on. Have them do this individually and then in small groups, and then see whether the total group can reach a consensus.

Close with rereading of the commandments studied.

The following are the contents of the envelopes and boxes, the position statements, and any special instructions.

Commandment 1

Objects in Box
Aspirin, toy car, money, letter grade *A*, pieces of paper with words like *power, popularity*, etc.

Step A
Lid envelope. Open the box. Take out the objects. If each object were to represent a god, identify them and rank them in the order of importance in which you think your age group holds them.
Bottom envelope. Would this fellowship group rank them differently? Why? Have participants decide in total group, or in small groups first, and then report to total group.

Step B
Position statement. The commandment, "You shall have no other gods before me," means that anyone who owns a Rolls Royce or Mercedes is not honoring God.

Commandment 2

Objects in Box
Bible, cross, flag.

Step A
Lid envelope. Open the box. Take out the objects. (1) What might these objects sum up, stand for, symbolize? (2) Choose one object. Rip it, break it, or tear it up.
Bottom envelope. (1) Why did/didn't you decide to rip, break, or tear up the object? (2) Discuss with the group how you felt about your decision. Would they have acted differently from you?

Step B
Position statement. The commandment, "You shall not make for yourself a graven image," means it is a sin to try to paint a picture of Jesus.

Commandment 3

Objects in Box

A coin, a picture of poverty-stricken Americans, and a quotation (see Step A below).

Step A

Lid envelope. Open the box. Remove the objects. Read the quote.

> *Someone once said that people really "take God's name in vain" when they don't take God seriously. This may mean people swear because they are not serious about believing in God. It might also mean that people who call themselves Christians and do not take their faith seriously are taking Christ's name in vain. The person who claims to be a Christian and hates his or her brother or sister, who does not help people, and who is not open for love in his or her own life— well, that person has taken Christ's name in vain.*

Read what the coin says about God. Show the group the picture of the poor people.

Bottom envelope. Thinking about the coin and the picture, name three ways—ask for help if you need it—in which we take God's name in vain.

Step B

Position statement. Swearing is a good example of taking the Lord's name in vain.

Commandment 4

Objects in Box

Single-edge razor blades, styrofoam cups.

Step A

Lid envelope. Open box. Pass out the objects. Everyone is to carve the cup into what, for him or for her, honoring the Sabbath is ideally all about.

Bottom envelope. Ask each person to share his/her creation, placing all the cups into the center of the group. Discuss the results.

Step B

Position statement. Sunday is a day of rest. You should not work.

Note: If you plan to stop here and to resume the study at another meeting, move to Steps C and D, as previously described.

Commandment 5

Objects in Box

Picture of father or mother and son or daughter, pencils and paper for everyone if you are including the option (see below).

Step A

Lid envelope. Open the box. Remove the picture and card. Look at the picture. Assume it is a parent with son/daughter. Tell a short story about the picture. What led to the moment shown in the picture? What will be the outcome?

Bottom envelope. This card is to be passed around. Each person is to pick any of these lines and complete it aloud and may repeat the line as often as desired. When everyone has responded, share feelings and questions.

> *"I honor my father and mother when I _____ ."*
> *"I don't feel like honoring my father when he _____ ."*
> *"I don't feel like honoring my mother when she _____ ."*
> *"I think respect comes from _____ ."*
> *"They won't respect me when I _____ ."*
> *"I don't respect them when they _____ ."*
> *"I like to call God 'father' because _____ ."*
> *"I never use the word 'father' when I talk about God because _____ ."*

Option. If there is time, you may want to include this additional activity. Give each person paper and pencil. Participants now have five to ten minutes to write a letter to their parents with at least two paragraphs. One begins, "I wish that you _____ ," and the other begins, "I wish that I _____ ." These are not to be shared, but folks may want to discuss feelings about having written such a letter.

Step B

Position statement. Few people really honor their fathers and mothers.

Commandment 6

Objects in Box
    None.

Step A

Lid envelope. Read aloud this statement and the poem which follows.

> The Sixth Commandment is "You shall not kill." Albert Schweitzer felt this commandment encompassed all life and consequently believed that if he killed animals, he was disobeying God. He therefore was a vegetarian. John Donne believed God meant you should not kill humans, and he once wrote, "Any mans [sic] death diminishes me. . . ." Others, like Melvin Laird, believe God meant you shall not murder *people, and there they believe it is okay, even necessary, to have wars.*

> We Need Not War!

> There are those who say . . .
>   War needs to be—past,
>   Present, and future.

> But I say . . .
>   We need not war!

We have had our days and nights
  Of years
    Of bloodshed and hate;
We have seen life and love and hope
  Battered
    In those shattered times.

And sometimes they had names—
  My brother was killed
    My son crippled.

There is too little time
  To live, and give!
    Too few days and nights
    And years.

War is still here
  In you, in me,
    In our friendly neighborhoods.

Neighbors,
  What shall I tell my brother's wife?
  What shall I tell my son?

Please, please, no more war.

There is too little time,
  We need every day and night
  And year
    to live, and give!

I say . . .
  We need not war.
There is too little time. . . .
  We need not war!

        —An Anonymous Father

Bottom envelope. What are some of the things you would tell this man if you could send him a letter? After sharing a few things, divide the group into small groups to write a response to this man.

Step B

Position statement. Vegetarians are the only ones who follow God's commandment, "You shall not kill."

Commandment 7

Objects in Box
  None.

Step A

Lid envelope. Place two chairs in the center of the group and then, with two volunteers, role-play the following situation.

> THE MAN. You are Jim and you have just discovered Jane is pregnant. She is telling you some of her concerns but you want her to have an abortion. You don't want the responsibility of a kid! You are basically an okay guy, but you don't really feel a lot of responsibility for Jane either.
>
> THE WOMAN. You are Jane and you are telling Jim that you are pregnant by him. He doesn't seem to feel too concerned. He wants you to have an abortion and forget it. You aren't so sure, and you wonder how he could say he loved you and now be so cold.
>
> THIRD PARTY. Wait two minutes, then enter. You happen into the discussion between Jim and Jane, two friends of yours. They have been more or less going together for six months. You've known they have been sleeping together, and you're also sure that Jane is more serious than Jim with the relationship. You like both people. Obviously something big has happened. You'd like to help, as a close friend.

Bottom envelope. The woman role-player meets with all the males in the group and the man meets with all the females in the group to discuss the role-play. All are to try to see the viewpoint of the opposite gender, as well as state their own views.

If time permits, you might then consider repeating the role-play, reversing the characterizations so that the woman is unconcerned and ready for an abortion, and the man feels differently, responsible, etc.

Step B

Position statement. Dating is for fun, and responsibility doesn't enter into it.

Note: If you plan to stop here and resume the study at another meeting, move to Steps C and D, as previously described.

Commandment 8

Objects in Box
Piece of string, card marked "agree," card marked "disagree."

Step A

Lid envelope. In the box is a piece of string. Stretch the string out on the table into a straight line. Put the card marked "agree" at one end and the card marked "disagree" at the other end.

Bottom envelope. Ask the people in your group to listen to each of the following situations and then put something they can call theirs—a pen, ring, locket, piece of paper—on the string where they would place themselves.

> *(a) John saw his history teacher use the duplicating machine. John used the machine next and discovered a copy of tomorrow's test, which the teacher apparently had run off. It was an extra copy. His teacher would never miss it. John said to himself, "I'll be able to go sledding tonight and still get an A on tomorrow's test." Then, "I'll do it!"*
>
> *Would you agree and do the same?*
> *Would you disagree and turn the test in?*
> *Put yourself on the line. Then discuss why you put your objects where you did.*
>
> *(b) Mary was in the store and saw just the perfect necklace lying on the counter. No one was at the counter, so she walked over*

and, while pretending to look at some stuff on the shelf, dropped the necklace into her coat pocket. She thought, "It won't hurt them; they mark stuff so high anyway."

Would you agree? Disagree?

Place objects on the line and discuss.

Step B

Position statement. The commandment, "You shall not steal," made sense in Moses' day, but does not make sense today.

Commandment 9

Objects in Box

None.

Step A

Lid envelope. Explain this exercise to the group. You are going to whisper a story in the ear of the person sitting on your left. This person asks no questions, must listen and then whisper it to the person on his/her left, and so on, until the story finally returns to the person on your right. This person tells his/her version of the story. You read the original (following) and then open the bottom envelope:

> *At one of the basketball games at Bloom High School, a group of blacks and whites sat together in the stands, cheering their teams on to victory. After the game there were no incidents. All was peace and good will in the spirit of Martin Luther King.*

Bottom envelope. One of the Ten Commandments is "You shall not bear false witness against your neighbor." Analyze the two versions of your story. What do they say about rumors? What do they say about your group?

Step B

Position statement. Gossip never really ever hurts anyone.

Commandment 10

Objects in Box
Big sack of candies that can be individually distributed.

Step A
Lid envelope. Open the box. Remove the big sack of candy. You, plus the person on your left and the person on your right, will decide what you will do with the candies in relation to the larger group, then do it.

Bottom envelope. The three of you, plus two other volunteers, form a goldfish-bowl discussion. Work on the following question: How does this situation reflect on the commandment, "You shall not covet your neighbor's house; you shall not covet your neighbor's wife, or his manservant, or his maidservant, or his ox, or his ass, or anything that is your neighbor's"?

Step B
Position statement. Things are never as important as people.

Steps C and D
As previously described.

CHAPTER NINE

Pilgrimage

The Christian spiritual life becomes a matter...of
working out, with the guidance of the faith community,
the implication of our primary loyalty to the Realm
of God.

Suzanne Johnson
"Education in the Image of God"

We are beginning to relearn in our time what seemed to be common knowledge centuries ago, that people learn best by doing. The Christian story is the foundation of our heritage. Rational learning does have its place within the confirmation process, and the content of the story forms a part of the foundation of knowledge of the confirmand. But it is important to remember that for most people rational learning is not transformative and does not bring about a radical reorientation of the personality toward a new way of being.

Life at its base is designed to be sacramental, with a small *s*. Behind this statement there is the understanding that a sacramental movement is any time that a person and God come into and are aware of each other's presence. As a result of the encounter between the person and God the person comes away changed. Our task then as confirmation leaders is to help the confirmands *experience* the sacramental richness of life. The confirmand leaders structure occasions and invoke God's presence; this accomplished, the transformation of the life of the individual takes care of itself through the grace of God.

The confirmand will come asking, "Where in the world am I?" and "Why am I here?" The responses to this last question will range from the coercion of parents to their own choice. However, regardless of the choice, the church's answer is the same, "You are here because someone believes that living needs to have greater meaning and that you need to experience the claims of the faith in this regard." Or, to paraphrase Augustine, "God has created us to accept God's claim on us." Our task as leaders is to be the guide on the journey of discovery and acceptance.

The Christian life is a lived experience. Christ did not say, "Lay down your nets for an hour on Sunday mornings and come check it out." He said, "Lay down your nets and follow me." He understood that you cannot investigate a faith and then decide to have it or not. You *live* the life. It is a pilgrimage, a journey of faith. For the period of the confirmation experience we are asking the confirmands to join us on a pilgrimage. We are not requiring that they have faith to begin with, although many of them will. We are asking that they live the journey with us. As we ask this we need to be ready to accept the responsibility of being the spiritual guarantor or guide on the journey. The expectation is that their spirit will be formed and shaped by the experiences that they have along the way.

There are two ways in which this spiritual formation will proceed. The guide will have some control over the first. As leader, you will look for multisensory experiences that will help the confirmands more fully understand the Christian meanings of the mystery of life. This includes the sacraments, but also the process of covenantal life together, as well as wilderness experiences of self, wrestling with being claimed by and submitting to God, the power of prayer as a resource along the way, our own inner conflicts, this thing called sin, and how the ritual acts of the church speak to and help us to overcome our times of brokenness. Words like *baptism, prayer, God, confession, forgiveness and guilt, anointing, healing and brokenness, communion, faith and doubt,* are some of the more formalized ways we in the church name important things over which we have no real control. Here we rely on God, and this is the second way spiritual formation proceeds.

Life in and of itself is a journey or pilgrimage. We do not and cannot create the journey. At best we can endow the journey with a specific sense of meaning. Thus, the journey that is the life of the confirmands—particularly in *community*—becomes the most salient material with which we have to work. And, in some ways, it is the easiest, for we do not need to worry about how to generate the experience to which we will add meaning. In this way we are helping the confirmands to *think theologically about their lives*. We help them create the tools they will need to take on their journey that will make it more meaningful. We can take their anxieties about drugs, sex, AIDS, intimacy, war, disarmament, gangs, and the occult, and turn them into experiential learning laboratories for theological education.

Experience 11: The Water of Life

Introduction
The sacrament of baptism comes to us from Jesus Christ. This session deals with the various symbolisms of the sacrament, how it originated, and what meanings it has for us today. Through a study of water and an experiential moment of forgiveness, the confirmands may come to a clearer understanding of baptism.

Purpose
Confirmation programs often must deal with some youth who have not been baptized. Through a brief background discussion and an experience with the use of water, the confirmands come to a better understanding of the biblical symbolism of water, as well as a new way of looking at baptism. This session presents the various understandings of the sacrament of baptism so as to let the youth actually "feel" the water and know God's grace and forgiveness.

Setting
This may be done anywhere, including a traditional classroom setting. Everyone should participate, but a spiritual "guide" serves as the one who articulates God's forgiveness. (This will be elaborated upon below.)

Preparation/Lead Time

The majority of the time needed to prepare for this session is devoted to the spiritual guide's study of the traditional understandings of the sacrament of baptism. This is necessary in order to lead the presentation of information and discussion at the beginning of the experience. Please be sure to consult your denomination's particular teachings and traditions related to baptism. The only other preparation needed is a basin of water and a towel.

Time

One hour or less.

The Experience/Process

1. Introduce the concept of "sacrament." A brief definition found in the Anglican Catechism says, "An outward and visible sign of an inward and spiritual grace given unto us, ordained by Christ himself; as a means whereby we receive this grace."[1] Again, please consult your denominational teaching on this. (5 minutes)

2. Lead a discussion, including questions and answers, in which the relevant information pertaining to baptism is understood by the confirmands. Include that baptism was instituted by Jesus when he said, "Go and make disciples of all nations, baptizing them..." (Matthew 28:19). Further Bible study might be found in one of the gospel stories of the baptism of Jesus by John (Mark 1, Luke 3, etc.).

Stress that baptism is a "sacramental" act. We see/feel the water, but we do not see God's grace. Neither do we see repentance, the faith of the initiate, or the community's acceptance. So baptism combines something seen with something unseen.

A possible definition of baptism is this: "In baptism, God imparts the gift of new life to people, receives them into fellowship, and welcomes them into the church family." An infant has vows taken by its parents, and God is said to welcome this child into a community of faith before the child can know about such things.

Adults often believe that in baptism God promises forgiveness (grace), and the person being baptized promises to lead a life of faithfulness. The traditional formula for baptism might also be included in this discussion, noting that a person is only baptized once, and you can't do it to yourself. It is an act of faith by a *community*.

This is a good point to enter into a discussion of the symbolism of water. It represents a cleansing (in a ritualistic way), drowning and rebirth, forgiveness of sins, and the down-pouring of God's grace. Water is such a common element, but without it we would die. It was especially needed by our first-century brothers and sisters, as it was a scarce commodity. Many take it for granted today: turn on the tap, and there it is.

3. One symbolism of adult baptism is that our sins are forgiven through God's grace. Have a basin of water and a towel on a table somewhere in the room. Explain that we are going to feel how water reminds us of God's forgiveness. *Be very certain to stress that this is not baptism that is taking place.* Ask each participant to think of a negative act they have committed in the past couple of weeks. This may be anything from treating people poorly to something more serious. These acts are to be thought about only, not shared with the rest of the group. After everyone has acknowledged that they have an act in mind, ask that a solemn mood be set in the room (perhaps light a candle). One by one, invite the confirmands to the table. The leader then does the following: (1) Ask the youth's full name; (2) say aloud that full name, saying, "[name], you are a child of God, and by God's grace, you are forgiven." As you do this with each confirmand, have them hold their hands over the basin, and gently let the water trickle through their hands as you say the words. The combination of feeling the water and hearing the words should serve as an assurance of God's forgiveness. Make sure all have ample time to come up to the table.

4. Discuss the experience. How did it feel to name an actual occasion when you hurt someone? How did it feel to know that you were forgiven? What were you thinking as you felt the water? What did you think about? Do you view water in a different way now? These are all appropriate questions for discussion. At the end of the session, say a prayer or sing a hymn of joy. (10 minutes)

Materials needed

Basin of water, towel(s).

So What?

It is hoped that through this discussion, and the experience of forgiveness, the confirmands will come to a deeper theological understanding of the sacrament of baptism. They should also feel renewed and restored as a result of the assurance that they are forgiven. By understanding water and its various symbolisms, we may all come to a new realization of something we take for granted. Perhaps the next time one of them takes a shower, goes for a swim, washes their hands, or takes a drink of cool, refreshing water, they may be reminded of God and God's ever-present grace.

Experience 12: Holy Ground

Introduction

When asked to recall some of the images informing our faith journey, we flip through a kind of photo album of the mind from which a series of "snapshots" rise to the surface of our consciousness. Most of the snapshots upon which we choose to reflect are powerful anchors for our faith. Even if we try to suppress some of the snapshots of our lives, they cannot be forgotten and rise into our consciousness. Some of these snapshots are disturbing, others are delightful, still others are mixed events in which part of the picture is not clear and remains fuzzy.

Purpose

This design provides the confirmands with several biblical texts chosen to provoke dialogue regarding several aspects of our faith journey, including awe/the holy, evil/sin, and grace.

Setting

This process could occur in the living room of a home, on a retreat, or in a classroom.

Preparation/Lead Time

There are four things to consider in the use of this design. (1) The confirmation leader/team must determine the appropriateness/inappropriateness of this design for those confirmands with whom this leader/team works. (2) A number of photos of persons covering a wide range of emotions should be clipped from magazines and individually mounted upon single sheets of construction paper. Pictures of persons in the confirmation group are not to be included. At least two photo choices per participant should be available; i.e., fifteen participants should equal thirty or more photos. (3) A camera can be used to take actual "snapshots" in this design. If this is to occur, the camera should be located and someone who understands how to use it should be ready at the correct time. (4) The process involves the technique of "body sculpture" a process in which participants are asked to assume physical positions in order to demonstrate emotions or certain vignettes taken from stories or parables. The leader asks a member of the confirmation team nonverbally to "sculpt" two or three other willing members into positions depicting alienation and joy. In this experiment, suggest that the two or three volunteers with whom the "sculptor" works are "human clay," and encourage the sculptor to adjust limbs, physically move persons into certain postures, and to move faces toward a smile or a grimace. As the experiment ends, ask the sculptor to join the sculpture, i.e., nonverbally to become a part of the human body sculpture. After this first attempt, consider how the experiment went. You will need to consider how best to use this technique with your group (if slightly older youth are peer confirmation leaders, having one or two of them volunteer for such a technique is a powerful mentoring experience for younger youth).

The Experience/Process

1. As the confirmands gather, ask that shoes be removed. If enough persons are in the group, arrange for two teams (using masking tape) to engage in building the "tallest" freestanding "shoe tower" in the world. Build the tower from teammate's shoes and masking tape. After appropriate measurements are taken, the

"winning" team passes out cookies and/or penny candy to all the confirmands.

2. If the group is large, retrieve both shoes, come together in small groups, and engage in naming some of the places this shoe has been. . . . "My shoe hiked in the mountains last summer"; "Jasons' shoe just returned from basketball practice"; "Amy's shoe visited her grandmother".

3. After everyone considers "where their shoe has been," ask the participants to reflect on where their shoes have been *in terms of their faith journey.*

On a long table, place photos clipped from magazines of individuals backed with single sheets of construction paper. Ask participants to wander around and to select and hold one picture with which they strongly connect, someone with whom they would enjoy talking with about their faith journey (where their "shoes" have been).

Suggesting that the photos selected by the group contain images of people who live real lives, who have joys and sorrows, who cry and who celebrate, the leader asks the group to respond to three biblical passages *as if they are the person in the photo which they have chosen.* Three passages are then read twice:

> Exodus 3:5. *Moses is busy tending sheep when he sees a bush that burns, yet is not consumed. As he approaches this burning bush, he hears the words, "Put off the shoes from your feet, for the place on which you are standing is holy ground."*
>
> Amos 2:6. *The prophet Amos expresses God's displeasure with those who profess to believe in God and yet perform evil acts. Amos asks, given such bad behavior, why is God angry? Because some people are willing "to sell the righteous for silver, and the needy for a pair of shoes . . . [in all this] God's holy name is profaned."*
>
> Luke 15:22-24. *The starving prodigal son, desperate to leave the predicament he got himself into, returns home feeling shame every step of the way, only to be greeted by a father who says, "Bring quickly the best robe, and put it on him; and put a ring on his hand, and shoes on his feet; and bring the fatted calf and kill it, and let us eat and make merry, for this my son was dead, and is alive again; he was lost, and is found."*

After reading these passages twice, write these summary phrases on the blackboard, or on newsprint taped on a wall.

Exodus: *"Take off your shoes, for you stand on holy ground."*
Amos: *"The evil sell the righteous for silver, and the needy for a pair of shoes."*
Luke: *"Put shoes on his feet, and let us celebrate."*

Instruct the participants, as if they *are the person in the picture they chose,* to offer a prayer to God (suggested by the photo and its interaction with Exodus, Amos, and Luke) written on the top part of the back of the photo. If needed, suggest a form:

Dear God,
  My name is _____ . This is what happened. I _____ . Now I am feeling like _____ . I pray that _____ . Would you _____ ?
    Sincerely,
    _____

Collect everyone's photo (with the prayers written on the reverse side). Shuffle the pictures, asking everyone to take photo not their own, and to suggesting their response to this person's prayer, *as if they are God.* If needed, suggest a form:

Dear _____ ,
  I hear your prayer, and I _____ . From what you said, I feel _____ . My hope is that _____ . I suggest you _____ .
    Signed,
    God

Again, collect the pictures (which now have a "prayer" and a "response from God" on their reverse sides. Shuffle the pictures, asking everyone to draw a picture not previously held by them. When everyone has drawn an appropriate photo, reflect as a group on what several of the photos/prayers/responses suggest.

At an appropriate time, reconnect with the three biblical texts; i.e., are there prayers of *awe* ("I am walking on holy ground")? Or prayers related to *evil-doing* ("I sold the needy for a pair of shoes")? Or prayers of *praise, joy, and celebration* ("let us make merry")?

4. Suggest that, having connected with the photos, the partici-

pants might produce a series of "snapshots." For example, several volunteers whose photos connected with the "burning bush" passage might be engaged in a "snapshot" body sculpture around *awe*; the "selling of the needy for a pair of shoes" around *evil-doing*; the "let us make merry, for my son, who was dead, is alive" around *praise and celebration*. (See body sculpture directions on p. 121) If a camera is available, take pictures of each body-sculptured "snapshot."

5. When discussion is concluded, gather in a circle and share prayer.

Experience 13: Flooded Moments

Introduction

Have there been times in your life when there has been no firm earth to stand on, when the bottom has disappeared, when you were flooded, swept away on a vast, chaotic sea, riding the storm out by yourself, totally alone?

Have you reached out for help and no one responded, until one day, in a gesture of peace and love, someone came to your little bobbing spot and said, "I love you"?

And you knew the promise was real, the waters began to receded, green showed through, life was renewed.

Have you lived that moment? Is it an image you can live your life by? It is the simple story of Noah, the flood, the ark, and the dove which returned with a promise that the good green earth would soon be seen again.[2]

Purpose

A kind of dialogue can be encouraged to take place between the biblical story and "life-texts," i.e., *our* story. The confirmation team/leader can offer (1) an environment of safety so that "my" story will be honored, (2) the choice of appropriate texts for a particular occasion, and (3) an openness to the possibilities of the resultant *dialogue*. In this design, there is assumed, on the part of the confirmation leader, a willingness to hear—in an appropriate, safe way—the personal "flooded moments" of participants in confirmation. There is assumed, on the part of the confirmands, a desire to "tell *my* story" in such a safe place. There is also the assumption on the part of the designer of this process that the "ritual dialogue" engaged in here is a potentially powerful *religious* experience.

Setting

Dependent upon how confirmation occurs, this could be visualized as a retreat worship, a classroom lesson, or the reason why the group has come together for a special afternoon or afternoon confirmation event. What is needed, in any case, is a comfortable environment in which people can assemble in a circle and focus on the activity in the center of the circle.

Preparation/Lead Time

Leaders should experience, prior to leading this session, what it means to engage in the technique called "body sculpture" (see p. 121).

Someone will need to have collected a set of magazine pictures of people who are experiencing flooded moments. If, at the time you run your own experiment in body sculpture, you also have on hand a stack of old magazines, it is a simple matter to discover at least two pictures (of persons experiencing flooded moments) for every one confirmand. These pictures are clipped from the magazines for use in activity 1 of this design.

The Experience/Process

1. Cover a long table with the magazine photographs that capture people experiencing the feeling of being "flooded" or "wiped out." Play appropriate music (sad, moody) in the background.

Ask participants to choose one picture that intrigues them. When everyone has a picture, the group reflects on what feelings are contained in the pictures.

After the pictures have been shared, ask for two volunteers. These two volunteers are, nonverbally, to move the entire group into positions and expressions that capture the feelings just shared. This body sculpture will result in people sitting on the floor, turned out, curled up—generally in a pattern of brokenness, alienation, and loneliness.

Ask the sculptors to assume positions as part of the living sculpture.

Ask people to "get into" what they are feeling, explore it, name it deep inside. Give a minute or two for this.

With folks still in their positions, read Noah's story (Genesis 6:11-14; 7:1-5, 11-12, 17-24).

2. Invite the participants to get comfortable but not to move from their spots. Pass out paper and pencils and ask them to write about a moment in their lives then they were "flooded." Following are examples from a ninth-grade confirmation program.

"I got flooded in school; everyone had already gotten into their groups and nobody wanted anyone else. I was truly flooded when I couldn't get into one of the groups."

"When I got suspended from school for drugs, and me and my friend had to talk to the pigs and the principal and it was their word against ours. They didn't take our word."

"The most flooded time of my life was a period of seven months in which I lost my grandmother, my best friend, and three other friends—all through death, which was too final; there is no undoing of it to find each other again."

"Our dog kept running away so we had to get rid of it. I thought with our dog gone it would be the end of the world. And when I saw the truck pull away with my best friend in it, I felt the whole world had turned against me."

Ask participants to share their flooded moments. If your group is large, you may wish to break into cluster groups for this sharing period.

Then ask whether folks believe that after or with each flood comes a dove with a twig of green hope. Has that been their experience thus far? If so, how has it happened? Have they ever been the twig of green hope for someone in a flood? Discuss.

3. If there is enough time, ask the group to form a list (on newsprint, chalkboard, poster board) of the kinds of things, concepts, and ideas they would want to take with them to help ride

out a flood. Here are a few examples, but let the list come from the whole group: The desire to live, a pet, a locket, love, a faith in God, life, understanding, memories, friends, one true friend, fun, a few jokes, a turquoise ring, music, my pain, my poems, inner strength, things I learned from a friend, the eyes of a child, the *Complete Works of Robert Frost*.

4. If the group members have remained in the sculpture-spots assigned by the two sculptors, fine. If not, ask them to resume their positions.

Ask one person to play the dove and to resculpt the group from alienation and brokenness to reconciliation and wholeness. It is imperative that the "dove" reposition everyone in order to complete the ritual dialogue. One can assume the dove's sculpture will be some circle-form of touching people.

As this sculpture occurs, a reader would intone Genesis 8:6-12, 20-22. If time remains, verbal discussion of the connections made between body sculpture moments and the spoken biblical texts can present a powerful occasion.

5. Standing in this circle, the confirmation leader encourages a sharing of joys and concerns, concluding with a prayer noting the "doves" of our lives.

Experience 14: Meditative Prayer

Introduction

We all wrestle at some moment in our lives with the question, "How can I have a meaningful encounter with God?" For many of us that question was first stimulated through the example of another. We saw someone who believed in the power of prayer and whose life was enriched by their direct relationship with God. They seemed to be at peace because of their relationship, and we longed for that peace. The quandary for us as spiritual guides is how to reproduce an opening to that experience for our young people in an authentic way. This exercise works at demystifying that experience and showing the youth how they might begin a similar relationship, a relationship that will last a lifetime.

Purpose

To help the confirmands experience prayer as sacramental contact with God, an experience through which they may encounter the presence of the Holy Spirit and the power of grace.

Setting

In a room that can be darkened, large enough to accommodate the group comfortably without touching, the experience could happen either as a stand-alone program or as a part of a larger program experience, like a retreat.

Preparation/Lead Time

If your own belief in the power of practicing disciplined prayer life is not secure, you might consider asking one or two persons for whom it is within your congregation to come and work with you on this exercise. (*Note:* It is not your own level of discipline that is the key, but rather your belief in its usefulness.) You might even ask the youth whom they consider to be models of prayerful persons, and then invite these people to participate in this occasion.

You may want to refresh your own understanding of how to begin and practice a disciplined prayer life. There are many resources available. Two examples are *You: Prayer for Beginners and Others Who Have Forgotten How* by Mark Link, and *Celebration of Discipline: The Path to Spiritual Growth* by Richard J. Foster.[3]

Create a multimedia experience that is a guided meditation. A typical meditation might include meditative music, slides or filmstrip frames, readings that will focus the attention of the individuals both on the foundation of God's creative grace and their soul's movement toward God through prayer and meditation, and a section that directs the attention of the individuals on their current experience of sacramental encounter.

If you have the extra time, this is a fun exercise to put together with a group of three or four persons, including youth, allowing the group's creative energies to work together.

Look to your own music library, the library of the church, the youth in your group, the local hospice chaplain at the hospital, the local public library, and the local Christian bookstore for meditative music to be used in the background. Look in the same places for poetry and readings that highlight the purpose of the guided meditation and for slides or filmstrip frames that could be useful to meditate on. (You might substitute a large candle here.)

Outline the flow of the guided meditation experience, coordinating the music, readings, and slides. Work at weaving a whole cloth from the many pieces. Practice it at least once.

Time

One hour

The Experience/Process

1. Open with a brief discussion of the meaning and purpose of prayer as the youth currently understand it. (5 minutes)

2. Continue with an explanation and discussion of some of the more traditional understandings of the meaning and purpose of prayer, being sure to emphasize its sacramental potential, its interactive nature, and its place in a lifelong faith journey. (10 minutes)

3. Invite the youth to write down what they currently believe prayer to be, including its process, power, and purpose, and the doubts that they have about it. (10 minutes)

4. Have the group gather to experience the guided meditation. You might have them all sit watching a screen, sit in a loosely formed circle around a candle or lying in a loosely formed starburst on the floor using the ceiling as the screen. In each case, have them sit or lie with enough space so as not to be distracted by each other. Be sure that they all have their sheets about prayer with them.

5. Let the meditative music and readings be long enough to create a mood of meditation and some mental images behind the experience. Then move to the section that directs the participants' attention to their current experience or sacramental encounter. You may want to use music in the background here, too, but not a visual image. An example might be as follows (10 minutes):

> Now close your eyes and imagine that you are sitting on a field
> which is familiar to you, where you feel safe. [Pause—in each in-

stance pause long enough for the listeners to actually have the imag-
ined experience you have suggested.] Notice what it feels like, smells
like, and sounds like to be there. [Pause] You turn around and notice
that there is a large knobby hill behind you. Something draws you to
go and explore. [Pause] As you go you pass trees and a meadow
[Pause], a babbling brook [Pause], animals and birds playing around
you [Pause], and you come upon a path going up the hillside. You
take it. [Pause] You come out in a rocky clearing. [Pause] There is a
strange light coming from around the next bend in the rocks. It is
warm and inviting. [Pause] You turn the corner and bask in the
light's warmth. [Pause] You realize that you are standing in the
presence of God. The light seems to come from everywhere and yet
nowhere. You walk forward, offering your prayer sheet to God.
[Pause] Listen, God is saying something. Experience the richness of
God's presence. [Long pause] Now, return to the valley by the same
route you came up. Thinking about what you experienced in God's
presence. [Long pause] When you get back to the valley you sit back
down and rest. [Pause] Then, when you are ready, come back into
this moment and open your eyes. [Continue with the music and the
darkened room long enough for all persons to come back into the
present and to savor the experience.]

6. Invite the youth to share what the experience was like for them. (If you have a group of more than twelve, you may want to divide into smaller groups with a leader in each group.) Encourage them to use all their senses. The intensity of experience will probably be fairly diverse. You will want to affirm this diversity and the appropriateness of each unique experience. (10 minutes)

7. Invite participants to share what they felt and heard as they imagined themselves in the presence of God. You might add to the discussion here how God can use our natural gifts of imagination, intuition, and intellect in God's relationship with us, especially in prayer and meditation. (5 minutes)

8. Close with a corporate prayer, standing and holding hands in a circle. Encourage all to participate, but allow the freedom to choose. (5 minutes)

Materials Needed

Pencils and paper for everyone, slides, music, readings, sound equipment, projectors as you have decided to use them.

So What?

Begin with a functional definition of a sacramental moment as any moment in which a person is aware of God's presence and where the person comes away changed as a result of the encounter. Then any moment and life in general can be seen as potentially sacramental. If one goes further to say that life is designed to be lived in harmony with the divine will and that we as created beings long to be reunited with God, then life itself is designed to be sacramental. Yet, much of our life is lived with little awareness of God's presence.

We strive as spiritual guides in confirmation to generate experiences that will help prepare youth to make a commitment to a life of Christian faith. By helping youth understand that prayer is an encounter where God is actually present in the experience, we help prepare them for a faith life that can be sacramental at its base. It is often helpful to remember that Christ himself frequently pulled back away from the crowds to pray. There was a need even in the life of Christ, who lived as one with the will of God, to stay in sacramental contact with God. How much more then do we, who continually fall short of that goal, need that same life-giving and life-changing contact?

Experience 15: The Letter

Introduction

The power of the Lord's Prayer is often lost amidst rote memory and a lack of awareness as to why the prayer was initially needed. We all need ways of keeping it fresh so that it might remain a prayer of the heart and not simply a prayer of the head. We also need ways of praying that connect with how we experience the world.

Purpose

Help the youth understand that the Lord's Prayer is a practical prayer that focuses on everyday issues through experiencing one way of making it practical.

Setting

The youth's typical program space and room the adults in the church use as a lounge.

Preparation/Lead Time

Ask two persons if they will perform "The Letter." (See appendix B for script.) Most persons need at least two weeks to memorize a seven-minute play (this will vary).

Be sure to (re)familiarize yourself with the commentary material on the Lord's Prayer passages in Matthew and Luke, focusing on why Christ may have felt a need for such a prayer.

Time

One hour.

The Experience/Process

1. Introduce the session with a brief summary of why Jesus may have felt the need for a prayer for the people. (5 minutes)

2. Break into subgroups of five to seven persons each, giving half of the subgroup the Matthew 6:5-15 section, and half the Luke 11:1-4 section. (It is helpful to use different translations.) Have the groups read their sections, the corresponding commentary pages (noting key ideas on paper), and then discuss the question, "Why might Jesus have taught this prayer to his disciples?" (15 minutes)

3. Invite the groups to follow you to the "lounge" to view a play that will add to their discussion. Begin by having the group brainstorm ideas for why people pray (recording the ideas on newsprint). Hush the group discussion as the lead character comes in the room, letting them eavesdrop on the play in silence. After the play, distribute pencils and paper to the group and have each person write down some ideas of what they might include in a letter to God. Have them use the different lines of the Lord's Prayer to stimulate their thinking about themselves.

4. Return to the youth room (silence is often very effective here), and return to the small groups to discuss the play and their responses. Hand out copies of the play so that they can refer to it as needed. Following are some possible questions (15 minutes): What are your initial impressions? What are some of the ideas you wrote down that you might put in a letter to God? What are you now considering about the Lord's Prayer that you had never thought of before? How does this relate to what you read in the Bible and commentaries before you saw the play? How might this change how you feel when you say the Lord's Prayer in the future?

5. Regroup as a whole for a summary time of what had happened in the small groups. (5 minutes)

6. Standing close in a circle, hold hands and pray the Lord's Prayer together.

Materials Needed

Bibles of different translations, a few commentaries of Matthew and Luke (one for each 5–7 people), pencils, blank paper, and enough copies of the play that everyone can work on their own copy.

So What?

The Lord's Prayer often becomes a prayer we say from memory with little conscious consideration of what we are saying. In some churches, spontaneous prayer seems to continue to decline in its frequency of use. Thus, we as leaders have the task of returning the Lord's prayer to its conscious status within the lives of the persons with whom we work and encouraging them to use various forms of prayer in meaningful ways. It would seem, given our current knowledge, that Jesus faced a similar problem, that of helping the people to have meaningful contact with God through prayer amidst their feelings of inadequacy. His use of prayer was in contrast to the showy prayers of the temple and street corner that tended to lift up the person praying more than the contact made with God. In response to the feelings of the laity that they could not approach God, the Holy One, the Lord's Prayer gave common folk access to God and a way to begin. It would seem that in our own time as the prayer has become a rote exercise that we have also lost much of our fear of approaching God through prayer and our ability to use prayer as a means of meaningful contact. We need now to help bridge the gap between unconscious recitation and fearful avoidance to a place of conscious respect and interaction, humanity and grace.

Focus Event on Pilgrimage: Christ's Claim

Introduction

An overnight "lock-in" can be framed as a spiritual "trek," given the concerns of contemporary youth and the potential claim of Jesus on their lives.

Purpose

There are many nets within contemporary culture poised to snare us. This interlocking series of activities is designed (1) to uncover some biblical criteria for groups open to Christ's invitation, (2) to reflect on some of the cultural snares and "nets" we encounter in North America, and (3) to name appropriate boundaries for this particular group in this time and place.

Setting

This is an intensive overnight experience, best realized as a "lock-in" at a home church. Because sleep will be minimal, Friday evening (during school season) is preferred. Participants should bring a sleeping bag, pillow, small amount of money to defray food expenses, and willingness to "work" from 7:00 P.M. until 2:30 A.M. From 3:00 A.M. until morning, areas are set aside for sleeping and for talking/music/playing. No one leaves the building after 7:00 P.M. entry. Everyone is picked up by 10:00 A.M. Saturday.

Preparation/Lead Time

Slightly older youth can play a key role and help plan and facilitate this overnight. If such persons regularly assist in confirmation, utilize them to their fullest capacity on this occasion. Details of the overnight should be mailed to parents (with lock-in rules explained) in advance, and local police should be apprised that youth will be up late in the church the night of this event.

The Experience/Process

Activity 1

Entering participants receive, around their neck, a construction paper "fish" on a yarn loop. This symbol is not explained at that time. All questions are diverted with the response, "We'll explore this later tonight."

Activity 2

Depending on the number of participants, groups can be determined (three to six per group) by cutting any or all of the following scripture sentences into pieces (which are then drawn from a hat and reassembled). Let's say, for example that eight youth arrive for the overnight. A decision is made to form two groups of four youth each, plus one youth staffer and an adult advisor. A scripture sentence is written on construction paper and cut into six pieces. Two pieces are given to the staffer/advisors, and the remaining four are placed in a container from which, after the second sentence is "cut up," all youth participants draw a piece of a sentence and then match it with other pieces until a correct sentence emerges. Following are some sentences:

> *Verse 5 from Romans 12:1-8: "We, though many, are one body in Christ."*
>
> *Verse 26 from 1 Corinthians 12:21-31: "If one member suffers, all suffer together; if one member is honored, all rejoice together."*
>
> *Verse 4 from Ephesians 4:1-6: "There is one body and one Spirit, just as you were called to the one Hope that belongs to your call."*

Activity 3

As groups identify their sentence, they should move to a comfortable space and reflect on both their organizing scripture sentence and Mark 1:14-20. In this passage, Jesus asks some fishermen to "lay down their nets" because he "will make fishers of men."

Ask participants to identify some of the "nets" our world weaves that might ensnare us. Are these nets powerful? Why do persons willingly enter their snare? What do you think Jesus means about "laying down your nets and becoming fishers of men"? What about women? Check other translations. And does the organizing sentence (from Romans, 1 Corinthians, or Ephesians) mean anything important, given Christ's call to us? Bibles should be checked, with sufficient time spent with each passage for adequate reflection.

Ask each participant to use one side of the construction paper fish (worn around the neck) to complete these sentences:

I've discovered _____ .

I had reaffirmed _____ .

I still have questions about _____ .

If possible, those sentences could be written around the edge of the fish. In the middle of the fish a figurative image, stick figure, or picture might be attempted to encourage a visualization of God's "call," Christ's words, "Lay down your nets," or "We are Christ's Body."

Activity 4

While the Bible study occurs, one or two staff members set up, in an asphalt-tiled room or a church basement, a "maze" comprised of seven or eight cardboard "islands" (drugs, popularity, grades, money, power, sex, etc.) connected by "sticky-on-both-sides tape" in complex "traffic patterns."

When Bible study ends, ask for five or six volunteers, blindfold them, and instruct everyone else to observe while these persons "find their way" onto "security islands." Tell the participants that while only two persons can remain on any given island, there are enough islands for everyone to wind up on one by themselves. If two persons are on an island and wish to remain there, when another person arrives they are to assist that person toward a possible "exit." Several "exits" (sticky-tape patterns) are available for each island. *Note:* Depending on the energy level of the group, safety monitors (older youth who provide safety and help) might be needed. The maze winds up looking as shown in Figure 2.

This is what a floor in a room would look like.
There can be as many "islands" as make
sense for your group.

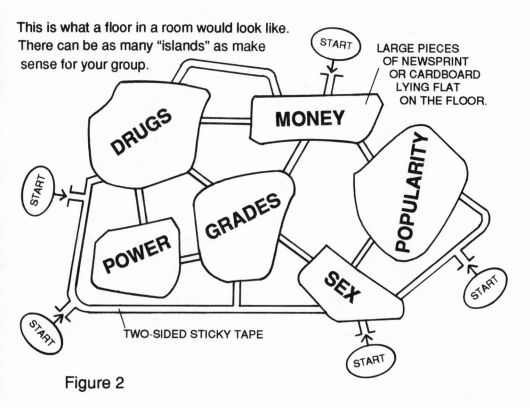

Figure 2

After every participant has landed on an island (no more than two per island), blindfolds are removed. Ask the following questions: How secure is your island? Is this what you hoped to achieve in life? Is this a snare, a net? Were there dangers on the way to your island? What problems happened once you arrived? Are such islands essential in real life? What issues are raised by Jesus saying, "Lay down your nets and follow me"?

Everyone might reverse the yarn fish around their neck and complete the same three sentences and devise a second symbol as was asked for at the conclusion of Activity 3.

Activity 5

Break the routine with a snack and/or "Sardines." "Sardines" is a hide-and-seek game with a slight twist. Instead of shouting, "I found them, I found them," the one who finds the hidden person(s) joins the hiders. A large group might choose three or four persons who must hide as a group. The group cannot move once they are hidden. The group has a maximum of five minutes to hide. Then everyone else searches. (This game necessitates the advisor checking out locked spaces and determining boundaries in advance of the event.) It is likely that you will complete only five "sardine" searches in three hours. *Note:* Decide in advance whether the first three to find those in hiding or the last three to find them will become the initial "hiders" for the next set.

Activity 6

After "Sardines," reconvene the group and reflect on what the expression *Body of Christ* means. Unroll a large piece of felt or something that could reasonably wind up as a banner someplace in the church. Indicate a large box of fabric scraps as well as scissors, glue, thread, and other decorations usable in the production (by everyone) of a personal fish which will be glued or sewn onto the banner (with personal comments) as part of communion later that night. Begin work.

Activity 7

Ask persons to bring sleeping bags to a place prepared for communion. Sit on the bags on the floor around a cleared space where the fish banner will be assembled. Sing several songs and repeat the several scriptures noted above. Invite participants to glue their fish onto the banner. Do not force, but welcome any verbal comments. Engage in prayer. Move to communion or, if inappropriate, either a "love feast" or the sharing of a single loaf of bread with appropriate commentary.

Activity 8

Move to (1) sleep, (2) talk, (3) table games, or (4) to a video, such as *Godspell*.[4]

Activity 9

For breakfast, try real food that needs some personal work (like pancakes).

Activity 10

Here a leader might have a simple feedback procedure using a set of three-by-five-inch cards. On one side participants should describe positive aspects of the overnight. The flip side is for suggesting what might be done better, changed, or dropped. Do not put names on cards. Collect the cards. End with prayer.

CHAPTER TEN

Ministry

> . . . a parish that forgets the poor cannot teach its adults
> or children to recognize the Lord in the breaking of the
> bread.
>
> Marianne Sawicki
> "Tradition and Sacramental Education"

"I belong." These two words have a powerful meaning for people and, more particularly, for adolescents. Merton Strommen, in his book *Five Cries of Youth*, surveyed seven thousand church youth in an attempt to discover what was important to them.[1] Coming up with five overlapping themes or "cries" of youth, Merton stated that the loudest of those five cries was the cry of "loneliness." Teenagers tend to have a lower sense of self-esteem when compared to adults. Today's continued stress upon individuality suggests the weakening of communal bonds. Adolescent loneliness often is the end result of a youth's not feeling integrated into groups of friends or organizations. Every person has the great need to be able to say, "I belong."

Adolescents struggle to find niches in their lives where they feel they belong. Team sports, clubs, church youth fellowships, scouts, service organizations, and groups of friends (cliques) all affirm this. The ongoing process of confirmation can also serve to let the confirmands know that they *belong* (or do *not* belong) at church. Confirmation, in this context, may be understood as a "welcoming home" celebration by the "people of God." The church welcomes the confirmands into its number and, whether implicitly or explicitly, says to the youth that they *belong*.

The actual Rite of Confirmation itself is understood as an opportunity for the people of God to make clear God's claim. We

141

become a people of God, not a person of God. And we *belong* in a community of faith. As far as participation in a congregation is concerned, we believe that expressing the faith of Jesus Christ is not done on an individual basis, for example, by locking oneself away in a closet to pray. Rather, it is expressed through participation in a community of believers who together reach out to the world to do God's work. The need for engagement in appropriate forms of ministry is an underlying message of confirmation. One becomes a person who publicly accepts the mantle of ministry, both within the community and in the vocation to which one is called.

Thus, in the actual Rite of Confirmation, the leader is understood as having a "priestly" function, as the one who celebrates the initiation of the youth into ministry. This often is named as both *confirming* and *commissioning*. Blessing each confirmand, serving first communion, asking the questions of faith at the confirmation service, preparing the teen for the rite, and passing the peace are all examples of this priestly function. In this fashion the pastor welcomes the new member into the ministry of Jesus Christ.

We believe that the congregation within which youth affirm their baptismal vows is a community of faith and that such a community will offer many occasions during which ministry is practiced and where the participation of its adolescent members is appropriate. The church that does not do this is not clear about the invitation it extends regarding full participation in the ministry practices of the faithful congregation.

The church that touches youth where they live will consider youth who have traveled, who have been confirmed as members of the community of faith as persons capable of serving as ministers in a variety of settings. It will confirm and commission into ministry.

Such a possibility is well anchored in church history. In the early church, "ministry" was defined by three Greek words: *diakonia*, *koinonia*, and *kerygma*. *Diakonia*, the Greek word meaning service, is the root of *diakonoa*, *diakonia*, and *diakonein*, words used in the New Testament in reference to the apostles, to every Christian, and to special ministries, respectively. There is, however, no term within the New Testament that gathers all who minister into one special group and those who don't minister into another. The New Testament notes different functions of ministry—teachers, bishops, deacons, presbyters, and evangelists—but expects *diakonia*, service, from everyone. H. Moltmann, in emphasizing Jesus as the one unique high priest, suggests that "the community of the baptized is the community of those who have been called. There are no differences here. All are called and commissioned."[2] All are to serve.

Today, within an understanding where church members, young and old alike, are called to serve as co-ministers, a ministry with youth begins with the recognition that those youth who confirm their baptism vows and/or who join a faith community should be encouraged to become involved in ministry frameworks both inside and outside the local church. For example, co-ministers who happen to be adolescents serving on a team with adults responsible for confirmation should be commissioned by their churches to serve their peers as guides, facilitating and teaching youth who have been called together as explorers of the twentieth-century wilderness.

But such a ministry is also the claim of our baptismal vows, and the *practice* of such ministry by the faithful church should be the occasion for confirmands to experience the full weight of this challenge to their vocation. It is with this understanding that the five designs and the focus event of this chapter are offered.

Experience 16: Making Golden Calves

Introduction

We "make gods" to replace cheaply the claims of God. The gods we make may be called "popularity," "power," "money," or something else. The god most easily recognized is the god of material possessions. This could be our "golden calf."[3]

Ours is a consumer, "across-the-counter" culture. From our birth, the advertising world inundates us in a calculated effort to convince us that the products it praises will save us by meeting all our needs.

We should laugh at this, but a lot of our laughter is anxious laughter. Ads are powerful in that they prey upon our growing anxiety—anxiety that people won't like me unless I use *this* mouthwash, *that* deodorant, ride *this* motorbike, wear *these* clothes, and drive *that* car, or *have* this woman/man.

Purpose

Ads suggest hidden values. These values can drive us or, like tigers in the wilderness, devour us. Ads can be indicators of what we worship in our society and point toward our culture's ultimate concerns. But ads assume inner knowledge; in other words, the viewer/reader/listener must decode the ad's message, usually at an unconscious level. The purpose of this exercise is to raise the decoding process to a conscious level and to engage that conversation with a biblical point of view. As the implications of ads are understood, their seductive power is diminished. This session should occur with an *intergenerational* set of participants.

Setting

This experimental process could occur in an open hall space where people can move about. It must be intergenerational. The environment should encourage gathering "around" a golden calf.

Preparation/Lead Time

Note: This process involves a number of people working in advance to create a very large, blocky, waist-high papier-mâché animal using the following instructions.

To make the golden calf, use a sawhorse as a skeleton and tack chicken wire to it to form the bulk of the figure. On one end of the sawhorse, tack an upright T-stick to use as the skeleton for the neck and head. Then add chicken wire to form the neck and head. Papier-mâché is torn strips of newspaper applied to the chicken wire after being immersed in a cheap glue. To make the glue, mix flour and water to the consistency of a heavy cream. Cover the chicken wire with several layers of paper dipped in the flour glue. Create some features for the head by pinching together wads of glue-soaked paper or adding lumps of clay and then covering the lumps with strip layers of papier-mâché.

You should now have a rather ugly, sticky beast. Once dry

(overnight), it should be painted with a wall sealer paint. It will look better, but not much. Hide the finished beast. You will bring it out at the end of activity 1.

The Experience/Process

1. Entering participants discover tables covered with magazines and newspapers. Ask each person to rip out five ads that are appealing, using the criterion for selection, "I'd get/do this if I could."

Then each person selects from these five, the one ad that he or she would most like to get/do. Tell each person to "write a fantasy paragraph as if you had whatever the ad is selling. Write it in the first person—how it feels, tastes, smells, sounds *to you*."

Then, "In one short sentence sum up your fantasy paragraph." This is important. Everyone will need this short sentence.

Next, have everyone bring the ad, fantasy paragraph, and short sentence and gather into a circle.

2. Introduce the golden calf by telling the first part of the biblical story (Exodus 32:1-6). Each person is invited to present their ad to the circle and glue the ad onto the papier-mâché calf, while reading their short sentence. (These short sentences may be written, using an indelible ink marker or laundry pen, onto the papier-mâché beast.)

3. When every ad has been glued onto the "calf," a spray can of gold paint may be used (be sure to have newspaper or a drop cloth on the floor) to highlight areas of the now "golden" calf. While this occurs, read Exodus 32:1-6 aloud with no commentary.

4. All participants "number off" from 0 to 9. The number is to be a cue for reading the sentences out loud. A leader counts backward from 50, and whenever a participant's number is called out, the participant is to read his or her sentence. For example, if the number 5 is chosen, the sentence would be read on numbers 45, 35, 15, and 5.

The leader suggests that at number 35 all stand, that by number 30 they begin to shout their sentences, and tells them to be aware that as the numbers decrease, the leader will speed up their sequence.

The leader starts the countdown very slowly, then begins to

speed up. When the sequence nears 15, the whole group will be jumping up and down around the golden calf, screaming their sentences.

5. The leader calls out, "10, 9, 8, 7, 6, 5, 4, 3, 2, 1, 0." With "9" a kind of frenzied chaos reigns! When no more numbers are read, people are encouraged to reform the circle and to sit and listen to the entire Exodus passage (Exodus 32:1-6, 7-8, 15-26). Discuss the passage and the ads that were glued onto the "golden calf." Ask the group to reflect on "what God is/what God is not." What does this say about modern living, our *vocations* (literally, our "calling") and the *practices* of this church?

6. At the end of the discussion, ask the participants to join hands in shared prayer. Conclude the prayer and break the circle.

Materials Needed

One papier-mâché "calf" (prepared in advance), newspapers, magazines, glue, scissors, indelible ink marker, one can gold spray paint, drop cloth or extra newspapers. The "calf" can be cardboard stapled to a tripod or something more elaborate, but it should resemble a calf.

So What?

By reflecting upon the lures of the larger world, persons within a caring community of faith can begin to correlate biblical images, their religious tradition, and their personal experience.

Experience 17: "Let My People Go!"

Introduction

We are all enslaved by certain things in life; by our bondage to these things, we are "tied up" and unable to experience true freedom. The only things which free us are the ability to trust others and trust God.

Purpose

This experience seeks metaphorically to demonstrate those times when we are in bondage, as were the children of Israel in

Egypt. Through involvement in a blind "trust walk" and experiencing the liberation after bondage, the youth see firsthand how trust in God and others frees us. The things that cause us to be in bondage might be lack of faith, the materialism of our advertising-oriented society, and of course, our capacity for sin. The process is designed not only to provide the experience of bondage, but also to know how it feels to be free through the love of God. It also raises issues regarding what we are called to do in ministry and in our vocations.

Setting

This session is best suited to the outdoors and should take place in a natural environment (woods, field, etc.). Since these things are rarely found near churches, it is suggested that this experience take place on a retreat, overnight, camping trip, or other outdoor setting. Nighttime is the most favorable time to do this, as being blindfolded is included as a central part of the process. Everyone in the group should participate, but one or two leaders are necessary to serve as "spotters" and guides.

Preparation/Lead Time

Before the session begins, enough time is needed to cut up old sheets for blindfolds for each youth and to tie a rope into loops which are large enough for each participant to put a hand through. One long rope is required, and knots are tied in it, so each youth has his or her own loop. The loops should be spaced about two feet apart.

It is also helpful to familiarize yourself with the story of the people of God in the book of Exodus. They were in bondage due to their slavery, as they had to work very hard to build the great treasure cities of the Pharaohs. Poor working conditions, not enough food or drink, and the unavailability of materials all contributed to the bondage of the people. In conjunction with this ancient slavery experience, encourage consideration of those things in our society that cause people to experience such "bondage." Examples might include competition, substance abuse, peer pressure, sexuality, poverty, money, and so on.

Time

Approximately 90 minutes.

The Experience/Process

1. Begin with a discussion of those things in life that cause us to experience bondage (see examples above). Allow the youth to come up with examples of such bondage themselves, and ask each youth to describe in what ways these things enslave us. Also include in this discussion a brief telling of the story of the people in bondage in Egypt. Be sure to include the various ways they experience bondage. (20 minutes)

2. Tell the group that they are going to experience bondage firsthand. Pass out blindfolds, and place the kids' hands in the loops which are tied in the rope. Care should be taken that the rope does not fit too tightly on each participant. The loops should loosely fit around each confirmand's wrist, so they may also hold onto the rope as they walk forward. Blindfolds should be worn only after all have their place in the rope line, with hands in loops. (10 minutes)

3. There should be a leader at each end of the rope line, with a flashlight, in order safely to lead the group on the trust walk. Explain that it is up to each participant to tell the person behind them what to do. This is where trust comes in. If there is a fallen tree to be stepped over, stairs to walk up, or low̲ ̲ ̲ ̲ging branches to be avoided, this must be communicated dow̲ ̲ ̲ ̲ ̲ line as each youth comes to that particular obstacle. Walk for about 20 minutes or so.

4. Conclude the walk outside the area where you will be meeting for your closing discussion. While the participants are still blindfolded, a leader must cut the rope halfway between each person. (Some groups cut the rope as part of a ritual in which the leader says, at each cut, "Whatever binds you, Christ frees you.") Be careful with this, and let the kids know what you are doing. After each person has been "set free," he or she may remove the blindfold and go into the meeting area. Instruct the participants that they are to leave the remnants of the rope on their wrists. Each person should be wearing an "ankh" on their wrists. The ankh is an Egyptian symbol that represents life, love, and freedom. Each

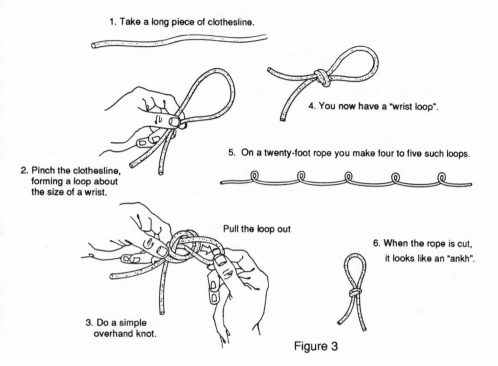

1. Take a long piece of clothesline.

2. Pinch the clothesline, forming a loop about the size of a wrist.

3. Do a simple overhand knot.

Pull the loop out

4. You now have a "wrist loop".

5. On a twenty-foot rope you make four to five such loops.

6. When the rope is cut, it looks like an "ankh".

Figure 3

cut of the rope will form an ankh for each person (see figure 3). (10 minutes)

5. Ask the youth how they felt during the experience. What was it like to be in bondage? Were the people around you helpful? What problems did you have? How did it feel to be blindfolded? Did any of you peek through your blindfolds or take them off? Be sure to make the connection between the bondage just experienced and the bondage of the people of God in Exodus. What are the similarities and differences?

Next move on to a discussion of how it felt to be released from captivity (by cutting the rope). Be sure to include a discussion of those things which free us from our bondage (God's love, trusting others, etc.). Discuss the significance of the ankh. Note that the Coptic Church saw the ankh as a cross and a sign of life. Talk about our "call" and how this connects with our "vocation" (literally, our "calling"). (25 minutes)

6. Offer a group prayer of thanksgiving to God, who sets us free from our bondage. Instruct the youth that they are to continue wearing their rope for the rest of the outing as a sign of their trust in each other and a sign of God's freedom-giving grace.

Materials Needed

Rope with loops tied in it, sharp knife or hatchet to cut rope, blindfolds for each youth, flashlights for leaders.

So What?

It is hoped that this experience will allow each participant to feel realistically the hold that bondage has on us. Through trusting others and trusting God's love, we find that we are not alone in our bondage and that it can always be driven from our midst. The experience of liberation will lead to a new understanding of how we must rely on each other and rely on God's goodness.

Experience 18: CROP Walk

Introduction

CROP walks are sponsored all over the country by Church World Service, the relief, development, and refugee assistance arm of the National Council of Churches of Christ in the U.S.A. to raise money for famine relief around the world.[4] (Any similar community walk for hunger relief could be substituted.)

Purpose

Participation will help youth experience the wider church through a nondenominational agency, participate in a large-scale mission event, feel the strength that comes through collective action, understand the issues around world hunger, and raise money to help alleviate the problem.

Setting

The setting begins at your desk, is taken into the youth room and sanctuary, and then moves out into the streets where the walk will actually happen.

Preparation/Lead Time

CROP walks happen at various times around the country. Once you know when the walk near you is happening, you will need to begin preparations about two months in advance. CROP is very good about helping you to get organized once you make the commitment as a group to be a part of the walk.

The Experience/Process

1. Write to CROP to find out where and when the walks are happening in your area.

2. Inform the regional coordinator that you are interested in participating in the local walk and would like assistance in preparing your group. That person will provide you with a local church coordinator's packet, which includes the following: a promotional time-line and how-to kit, promotional materials, sponsor sheets, an order form for movies, videos, and program aids, and all of the details that you will need to coordinate the walk for your church.

3. Two months in advance you will begin to promote the event throughout your congregation and youth group. (Intergenerational walks are the best kind. Encourage adults in the church to walk with the youth.)

4. Plan to devote at least one group meeting two to four weeks in advance to the theme of world hunger and the upcoming walk event. The advance programming is a major factor in whether or not the youth personally own the event and see it as more than just a walk. You may want to take this opportunity to do a series of group programs on world hunger issues.

5. Plan to have a great day and for the walkers to want this as an annual event in their program. Your attitude can truly be contagious.

Materials Needed

A local church coordinator's packet, medical release form/permission slips, drivers and adult walkers (at least one for each seven youth).

So What?

Despite what happens in our world, food is the most precious commodity. It and water are the two main sustainers of life. Thus, CROP walks are about hunger, but they are also about justice, world peace, and the simple mandate of Jesus to love each other as God has loved us. Adults and parents will often ask, "Why walk, why not just donate the money?" The answer is simple. By gathering sponsors and then actually walking in a crowd, the young people experience the power of faith in action. The giving of time is often far more sacrificial than the giving of money for both adults and youth. Thus, the solidarity that is experienced between the walkers and between the walker with the cause is enhanced. (It is often helpful to parallel this event with a work event later in the year where the youth actually see the faces of the people they are helping. There is nothing quite like feeling that what you are doing really makes a difference in someone's life!)

Experience 19: The Church with Its Sleeves Rolled Up

Introduction

We can say that congregational mission is the body of Christ expressing Christ's concern for others. By serving others we are involved in worshipping God and acting as caretakers and stewards of God's world.

Purpose

This experience offers the confirmand a hands-on experience at serving others; that is, the strangely warmed heart one gets from helping others and the frustration one feels when one realizes that the poor will always be with us.

Setting

Service can be performed in a soup kitchen, mission, etc., at any time of the year. A service project should be required of all the confirmands.

Preparation/Lead Time

A great deal of planning is needed for a full-blown work week. Allow nine months for the whole process. Consult your denominational office and/or local pastors for information on choosing a site and planning a work week. For a shorter experience (soup kitchens, etc.), a six to eight-week lead time should suffice.

Time

One day or one week.

The Experience/Process

1. Introduce the ideas of worshipping God by serving others to the confirmands. Ask them to look up and explain various Bible passages which relate to this theme. (Matthew 2:13-17 and 25:31-46, Amos 5:21-25, Luke 10:25-27 and 22:24-27, and Galatians 3:10-12 are a few examples.)

2. Discuss how we as Christians could live out these teachings. Have handy the names and descriptions of missions, soup kitchens, and so on in your town at which the confirmands could work. Individuals or small clusters might commit to spending a day at one or two of them. We believe such experiences should be regularized, e.g., *every* Thursday or *every* Saturday.

3. Have the group share their experiences, both their "successes" and frustrations. Conclude with a prayer.

Materials Needed

Bible.

So What?

Service projects are often, in retrospect, transformative "mountaintop" experiences for participants. They offer Christians a chance to express Christ's concern for others and are essential aspects of any faith-filled community. Service weeks are time-consuming to plan and lead, but they are worth every minute of it.

Experience 20: A Children's Ward

Introduction

This session suggests entry into one of the ongoing ministries of a church. We place it here with the awareness that one such visit is inadequate. If the church is engaged in a regular ministry, however, this session makes sense. In any case, an explanation of why they are making this visit needs to be determined, as well as information about some of the medical conditions of the children they will be seeing. In certain instances, chaplains and/or medical personnel can orient the confirmands; the leader ought to engage the group in theological and spiritual reflection after and during the visit.

Purpose

It can be very humbling for youth to visit other youth in the hospital. It will help them to put issues in their lives into some perspective while helping them realize that their own good health is nothing to take for granted. It may also raise deep questions about life and death and should encourage a feeling of reaching out for the youth, to focus on others and decide what they might do to help. It will also raise questions like how and why the church does this ministry of care.

Setting

Leaders will need to confer with the hospital as to the best time for the patients, probably a Sunday afternoon. All youth and youth leaders should visit.

Preparation/Lead Time

Make the arrangements with the hospital first, then arrangements with parents for drivers (meeting and returning from a central place, probably the church). Prior to leaving, patient information should be shared.

Time
Two and one-half hours.

The Experience/Process
1. Share patient information, explanation, and orientation. (10 minutes)

2. Once at the hospital, meet with the contact person, and have the youth separate into pairs to visit different rooms. Plan to have some books or games to play with those patients who are able. (Twenty-minute visits by each pair, then they switch patients; each should be able to visit four different rooms in the 90 minutes).

3. Discuss reactions and feelings upon your return to the church. (20 minutes)

Materials Needed
Games and/or books, coloring books and crayons, for example.

So What?
It is hoped that this experience will get the youth to think outside of themselves, to reach out and care for those who are in need, and ultimately to confront their own mortality.

Focus Event on Ministry: A Footwashing Experience

Introduction
Jesus washed the disciples' feet at the Last Supper as an example of his servanthood as well as a teaching tool to show them they ought to serve others (John 13:1-17). We, as Christians, are to serve others in the same manner. Involving the confirmands in a footwashing experience is a valuable experience in servanthood.

Purpose

This session's focus is two-fold. First, it is intended to form community among the members of the confirmation group through the use of a traditional worship setting. Second, the session allows the confirmands to experience the meaning of servanthood.

Setting

In no way should this experience be used during a typical confirmation group session. Much time and interpretation is required, as well as the hope that a solemn atmosphere will be present. It is suggested that a worship/footwashing take place on a retreat, overnight, bike hike, camping experience, or work camp setting. This experience is most effective at nighttime, after a day of learning and fellowship. Everyone should participate, but youth should never be forced to participate if they are too uncomfortable with the experience.

Preparation/Lead Time

The leadership should be well versed in the story of Jesus washing the disciples' feet found in John 13. Familiarity with first-century Jewish customs is also helpful in order to clarify the significance of this act was on Jesus' behalf. Feet were "unclean" by Jewish law, so washing the feet of someone, other than a child or family member, was to make oneself unclean. This is one reason the disciples were so ashamed that their Lord would lower himself to wash their feet. Consideration should also be given to the geographical setting. Sandals were worn as the customary footwear of the day, and animals were used for food, travel, and sacrifice. Thus we can assume that footwashing was an extremely unpleasant endeavor in this time, as the combination of exposed feet and the abundance of animal dung would imply. Jesus was not concerned about socks with holes or with athlete's foot, as we might be today. Rather, it was the ritualistic uncleanliness, coupled with the rather dirty and foul feet, that made the act so bold.

The leaders should also take note of the space which would best be used for this experience, as well as the mood of the group and where they are in terms of being able to take risks.

Time

One and one-half to two hours.

The Experience/Process

1. Explain all the historical and biblical interpretations of foot-washings (see above), and tell the group that they are going to be involved in a footwashing to conclude their worship. Be sensitive to giggles, questions, and an amount of uncomfortability at this point, and deal with these issues as they arise. The element of servanthood should be stressed throughout, and it is helpful to point out that it is much less threatening for us to do now than it was in the first century. (10 to 15 minutes)

2. Participate in the worship service. It is helpful if you have several older youth involved in the planning and leading of the service, so allow extra time beforehand to plan this. As the youth see their peers involved in the worship leadership, the footwashing becomes not something that the "adults are making them do," but a horizontally communicated activity.

Worship should include songs related to service and prayers, etc., that fit in with that theme. The most logical choice for the scripture reading would be John 13. As was the case with Jesus and the disciples, communion may be included in the worship if the sacrament is available to those who are not yet confirmed in your tradition. (30–45 minutes)

3. The footwashing may be done in several ways. Youth may do this in pairs, with someone to whom they feel a close bond, and the kids in each pair wash the other's feet. Another way is for the confirmands to sit in a circle and each wash the feet of the person next to them, passing the bowl and towel(s) around the circle as they finish. Lastly, the leadership may wash the feet of each youth, but be aware of this symbolism. We are attempting to show that we *each* must serve others. If the leaders do the footwashing, this shows that they portray the role of Jesus in a "Lone Ranger" fashion in which they serve as ritualist elders or priests. We suggest that the washing be done by all. (30–40 minutes)

4. Close with the singing of a hymn and a discussion that serves to debrief the experience. Ask questions such as, "How do

you feel after this experience?" or "What does this say to you about serving others?" Be sure to make the connection between the group's experience and what took place in the upper room many centuries ago. (10–15 minutes)

Materials Needed

Wash basin(s), water, oil or scent for water, towel(s), Bible. Optional: bread, wind, chalice(s), candles, words to songs.

So What?

By using this experience, the confirmands may gain new insight into the servanthood of Jesus as well as a new understanding of their call to be servants to others. A certain level of intimacy is involved in this session, as well as the possibility for discomfort or embarrassment. What this boils down to is taking risks. When we take risks of faith, we are aware of the risks that Jesus and his disciples took long ago. We are also aware that risk is always involved in the servanthood in which we are called to participate—the risks of missionaries in a new land, the risks associated with serving the hungry and homeless, or the risks of opening ourselves up in new ways to our peers.

It is also hoped that stronger bonds of community will be formed in the group as the result of both risk-taking and the level of holy intimacy that is a part of the experience. When we live in community, we serve one another, as Jesus taught, and this service makes the community come closer together.

CHAPTER ELEVEN

A Partial Review of the Literature: Confirmation Curricula in Theory and Practice

Researched by Timothy Nelson

Thanks to Ian Oliver and the Ecumenical Parish Resource Center at the Lutheran School of Theology, Chicago, Illinois.

Books and Articles

Dunning, James B. *New Wine, New Wineskins: Exploring the RCIA: Pastoral Implications of the Rite of Christian Initiation of Adults.* New York: William Sadlier, 1981.

Roman Catholic. Rite of Christian Initiation for Adults (RCIA). "The RCIA is about conversion, about the spiritual journey of the whole person (not just the cortex) to God. . . . The RCIA calls the entire community into mission, into sharing both Good News and their personal faith in the Lord" (10).

Dunning emphasizes the transmission of the Christian message as it has been passed on in the Catholic church. The curriculum centers around the church's life and its experience and expression of Christianity. He characterizes the RCIA image of confirmation as a spiritual journey which will last a person's entire life. This program can be run in nine months, but he strongly urges that people take more time. The suggested curriculum includes retreats and journal writing, and both laity and clergy are involved in teaching. Dunning draws upon research from developmental psychology, and he asserts that the RCIA tries to overcome the previous top-down orientation of catechetic instruction.

Gorrell, Brenda. *Six Designs for Local Church Confirmation Programs.* Prepared by Rev. M. Leysath, et al. Compiled for the Task Force on Confirmation Education, Division of Evangelism, Church Extension and Education of the United Church Board for Homeland Ministries, New York, N.Y., 1978, 1981.

United Church of Christ (U.C.C.). Six programs for confirmation of teens. Sample lessons, quizzes, and worksheets are provided. In all except the fifth curriculum, the emphasis is on content rather than faith development, as outlined below.

1. A five-day program taking place during a school vacation is modeled after a learning center. Students work on various topics (primarily theology and polity) using the resource materials provided. A few field trips are included. Students write their own creeds, and the diaconate examines the confirmands.

2. This program runs for twenty months. Eighth and ninth graders meet once a week for traditional classroom instruction with homework. The first year of classes covers the Bible and biblical theology. The second year involves liturgical theology (ecumenical) and church history, with emphasis given to the U.C.C. Students then take an oral examination on their faith. The third year is elective, with the students voting on the topics they would like to discuss.

3. This program lasts for two years, offering confirmands the option of being confirmed after the first year of confirmation instruction. The parents, confirmands, and the pastor all sign a confirmation covenant. Students must attend worship and prepare reports on what happened that particular week. They also must attend all classes and field trips, or make-up work will be assigned. There is a mission project at the end of each year, each individual must do service projects in the community, and the group makes a banner for their confirmation service.

4. Several churches combined their resources for this two-year program for seventh through tenth graders. There were three main retreats. Group sessions were held once a month for two and one-half to three hours, and individual churches supplemented them with their own meetings. The first retreat concentrated on commu-

nity building, self-identity, and the nature of confirmation. Local churches then held a covenanting service, and confirmands worked on Bible studies, sometimes using U.C.C. confirmation materials. The next retreat examined worship, and this was followed by sessions on prayer, grace, forgiveness, and sin. The last retreat focused on commitment, the Christian lifestyle, and the meaning of conversion. The program ended with an agape meal and confirmation.

Klos, Frank W. *Confirmation and First Communion: A Study Book.* Minneapolis: Augsburg, 1968.

Lutheran. Confirmation for teenagers. Klos reviews the reasoning behind the 1967 Lutheran study of confirmation. The book is a good introduction to Lutheran theology on the subject, and it presents basic issues in a helpful way. Klos points to four main emphases: (a) catechetical ("instruction," "confession of faith"); (b) hierarchical ("renewal of baptismal vow," "admission to Holy Communion"); (c) sacramental (reception of the Holy Spirit, can be mixed with the first two); and (d) *traditional* (catechetical, confessional, "intercessory consecration of the confirmands accompanied by the laying on of hands," communion could be taken before confirmation).

"Confirmation is a pastoral and educational ministry of the church that is designed to help baptized children identify with the life and mission of the adult Christian community, and that is celebrated in a public rite" (6). Klos adds that confirmation:

>—*is not a sacrament.*
>—*does not in any sense complete baptism.*
>—*is not a ratification of the vows or promises made by sponsors at baptism.*
>—*does not add any special form of God's presence or gifts that the baptized person does not already enjoy.*
>—*does not confer special privileges.*
>—*is not a prerequisite to Holy Communion.*
>—*is not essential to the Christian life. (142)*

"The Church must, therefore, equip the young person with the ability to recognize the need to adapt that [Christian] mission to his own time and to accept responsibility to it, using the resources which the church has received from the Holy Spirit" (149).

Lindberg, A. R., and M. J. Havice. "Catechetica Instruction: Using Media in Catechism." *Lutheran Partners* (September/October 1988): 30–36.

Lutheran. Use of videotaped resources in teenage confirmation programs. The authors conclude that a combination of video and workbook units for catechism would improve attitudes toward catechism itself and would increase the involvement of families in the process. Statistics and details from their study conducted in Wisconsin are also given.

Murphy Center for Liturgical Research. *Made, Not Born: New Perspectives on Christian Initiation and the Cathecumenate.* Notre Dame, Ind.: University of Notre Dame Press, 1976.

Roman Catholic. Rite of Christian Initiation for Adults (RCIA). This collection of eight essays deals with the historical, theological, and pastoral implications of the RCIA. A. Kavanaugh offers this summary of the Catholic view of catechesis:

> This [Christian] faith is no mere noetic thing but a way of living together; it is the bond which establishes that reciprocal mutuality of relationships we call communion, and it is this communion which constitutes the ecclesial real presence of Jesus Christ in the world of grace, faith, hope, charity, and character.
> This is what the eucharist celebrates, signifies, and causes within the community of the faithful: it is the church. This is what initiation in the fullest sense disciplines one for: it is the church. . . . Initiation defines simultaneously both the Christian and the church, and the definition is unsubordinated to any other except the gospel itself, no matter from what source other definitions may originate. (132–33)

Myers, Victor A. *Confirmation Ministry—A Family Life-Style: A Handbook of Resources and Ideas.* Lima, Ohio: C.S.S. Publishing Co., 1979.

Lutheran. Confirmation for teenagers. Myers believes that the following issues are involved in confirmation: content and tradition; lifelong processes; experiential aspects; family emphasis; clear and realistic expectations; concentration on belief systems; flexible programs; partnership of teens, parents, and church members; and clarification of "values in the light of the God-News Story" with "the accent . . . on process or experiential learning and content" (12).

The program model includes (a) required and elective courses held once a week (Bible study, catechism, applied Christianity over a three-year period); (b) attendance and participation in Sunday school, youth fellowship, worship services, and sermon review, feedback, and preparation; (c) service projects, field/work-study trips, working with church members; and (d) workshops for parents, such as Parent Effectiveness Training, marriage enrichment, etc.

Myers draws fairly heavily and explicitly from psychological models, especially the moral development theory of L. Kohlberg and J. Piaget. The formation is a primary concern of the author.

Roberts, William O. *Initiation to Adulthood: An Ancient Rite of Passage in Contemporary Form.* New York: Pilgrim Press, 1982.

United Church of Christ. Confirmation for teens. The first section of this book concentrates on rites of passage from psychological, sociological, anthropological, and theological perspectives. The remaining half of the book deals more directly with what Roberts sees as the underlying cause of our dilemma over confirmation: our even greater confusion about our teenagers.

Roberts describes his model of confirmation as "a two-year journey leading them to adulthood" (11). He vehemently disagrees with the "denominational executive" he quotes as saying: "In Christianity we confirm faith. We don't initiate people." The author develops the idea of confirmation within the broader category of initiation. He therefore stresses the person over the particulars of faith. Not surprisingly, Roberts lays out a curriculum that is far from anything resembling catechesis. The confirmands (about twenty eighth and ninth graders) meet approximately twice a week for two years, go to frequent retreats, and study, among other things, topics from the areas of society, self, sexuality, and spirituality.

Change is an integral part of the rite of passage. Roberts quotes a psychologist on the subject of liminality: "Several students of liminality have pointed out that one of the primary characteristics of this state is the capacity to see the self in new and broader and more appropriate perspectives" (20). He goes on briefly to describe initiation rites in other religions, similar rites in the Christian church, and biblical support of his argument.

Roberts is clearly more liberal than most other writers in this field. His paradigm is well developed and supported, but he draws more heavily than others do on the social sciences and materials that are not necessarily Christian. This could be helpful for some, but others will criticize that it is too secular. It is important because it offers a fresh vision for confirmation based on ancient traditions and is an excellent example of an alternative to the more ordinary confirmation curricula.

Smith, Kent L. "Confirmation." *Alert* (May 1983): 24–27.

Presbyterian. Confirmation for teens. Smith sees confirmation as a necessary and important theological and polity issue. He describes three basic types of structures for confirmation programs: the ongoing class, the one-shot event, and the individualized program. One's choice of programs needs to take into account the time and commitment youth can and/or will afford and the ages of the participants. Alternatives need to be offered so that the program can be tailored for different individuals. Youth in junior high will see confirmation primarily as a rite of passage to adulthood. Those in senior high will look upon it as "an act of faith and commitment" (27).

Thompson, George B., Jr. "The Milestone Project." *Nexus Notes* (Winter 1987).

Presbyterian. Confirmation for teenagers. Thompson asks, "How can we nurture a Christian 'life-world' that will become the primary source of meaning and relatedness for our children?" (1). The goal of confirmation should be, he says, to replace the cultural life-world with a Christian one. To do this, Thompson believes that the following elements need to be incorporated into the overall process of bringing youth into the church:

1. Knowing and interpreting the stories that give shape to the Christian life-world [biblical and catechetical units].
2. Participating in the rituals and ceremonies that give symbolic expression to the Christian life-world.
3. Experiencing the quality of relationships that reflect the understanding of persons in the Christian life-world.
4. Acting in ways that express the vision of the Christian life-world.
5. Structuring the life of the community as a concrete embodiment of the Christian life-world so that each person may share God's love, power and justice. (2–3)

These "key elements in the nurturing process" would take the form of greater parent/home involvement, Sunday school before/after worship, various ways for youth to participate more fully in worship, rituals that more closely tie together our "ordinary" lives with the sacred, emphasis on the celebrations and rituals of the church year, increased intergenerational interaction, and greater consideration of both global and local concerns.

Thompson hopes that the church can become what he calls a "normative organization . . . gathered around a shared vision" (7). In this way, "members become active as they are claimed by that vision and enabled to discover ways in which their own concerns are given expression in the organization's life" (7).

Willimon, William H. "Taking Confirmation Out of the Classroom." *The Christian Century* (March 16, 1988): 271–72.

United Methodist. Confirmation for teenagers. Willimon outlines four basic goals: (a) The goal of confirmation is discipleship; (b) we need to go beyond knowledge to belief and action; (c) we strengthen faith through experience, not intellectual knowledge; (d) we can use mentors to model and guide confirmands.

He describes one curriculum built around these points. The confirmand reads Luke and discusses it with a mentor. Worship, the church's budget, and polity, both local and denominational are all seen/experienced by both confirmand and mentor and then discussed. Other activities include a wedding and/or funeral and volunteer work in the community. Overall, Willimon says, we have to look at confirmation as a way of growing into the congregation instead of out of it.

Wingeier, Douglas E. *Confirmation Today: Ten Affirmations.* Nashville: Discipleship Resources, 1982.

United Methodist. This fifty-one page booklet outlines the history and practice of confirmation in detail. Though written for United Methodists, it is useful to most other denominations as well. Wingeier analyzes the present state of confirmation and notes that it continues to exist in a state of flux. Pastors and teachers desiring a detailed history of the practice and theology surrounding confirmation would do well to start here. The author does not suggest a curriculum, but the material here would help those seeking a deeper understanding of the rite and its role in the church. He includes a bibliography for further research.

Curricula

The two pieces in the marketplace most useful for the pastor at this time are The Presbyterian Church (USA)'s *Journeys of Faith* (Presbyterian Publishing House, Curriculum Services Department, 100 Witherspoon St., Louisville, KY 40202-1396) and William Willimon's *Making Disciples: A New Approach to Confirmation* (*The Overview, Mentor's Guide* and *Confirmand's Journal* are available from Logos Publications, Inc., 6160 Carmen Avenue East, Inver Grove Heights, MN 55076, 1990).

Presbyterian David Ng chaired the taskforce that put together *Journeys of Faith*. Five pieces are available, but the key purchase would be the overview, *Journeys of Faith: A Guide for Confirmation-Commissioning*. The materials come in loose-leaf format, and can be sorted, shuffled, and rearranged to fit the concerns of any size or format confirmation program. This material can be used with one confirmand. Specific materials ready-made for single group sessions as well as extended retreat sessions are uniformly helpful. Experiences in and out of "the classroom" are provided. The materials stress relationships, are sound theologically, and only have one section that concentrates on denominational concerns. Three small booklets orient the confirmand, provide a useful approach to studying Luke's Gospel, and present an interpretive overview to this confirmation approach for committees, educators, and pastors. This is an excellent resource for the confirmation leader and is highly recommended.

William H. Willimon's *Making Disciples* is a direct result of his working with the confirmation program leaders in his confirmation and their effort to discover a model other than the traditional classroom format to prepare youth for confirmation. Willimon asked what they hoped the confirmation process might do for the youth of the church, and their response (that persons who went through the process might have a more alive faith—like some of the church adults, in fact, had) caused Willimon and that group to jettison the classroom for a mentoring model that placed youth confirmands and adult church members into settings occasioned by the more natural workings of the local congregation. Willimon was so taken with the lively results of this experiment that he mentioned the model in his work with Stanley Hauerwas (*Resident Aliens: Life in the Christian Colony* {Nashville: Abingdon Press, 1989}) and eventually summarized the model in *Making Disciples*. Congregations using this approach note that initial enthusiasm often makes this a very lively and positive program, but that they frequently must struggle to discover new adult mentors after the initial crew moves on. Nevertheless, Willimon's approach is a powerful and viable option that many use in tandem with a modified classroom format. We strongly recommend it.

The following annotated materials are confirmation resources that cover several decades.

Affirm. Minneapolis: Augsburg Press, 1984.

Lutheran. Twenty courses over two to four years for early teen confirmands: (a) ten core courses of eight sessions each, two hours of study for four days per course; and (b) ten elective courses of four sessions each, one hour of study for four days per course.

The core courses cover both the Old and New Testaments, the Apostles' Creed, the Ten Commandments, the Lord's Prayer, the sacraments, Lutheran church history, Lutheran doctrine, discipleship, and worship. The elective courses touch upon such issues as the nature of confirmation, authorities, music, fairness and justice, emotions, prayer, biblical interpretation, hope within conflict, and honesty.

The goals of the *Affirm* series are as follows: (a) to understand the Bible and its message for life today; (b) to study the historical and biblical roots of the small catechism; (c) to learn the traditional doctrines of the Lutheran church; (d) to experience faith in relation to life's challenges; and (e) to respond to God's grace through prayer, song, praise, and witness and service to others (*Planning Guide,* 4).

The curriculum integrates the Bible, Luther's small catechism, worship services, and units on Lutheran heritage. It claims to be flexible in terms of when the classes can be held—weekends, weekdays, on retreat, at camp, etc. It is primarily content- oriented, with homework and memorization exercises to be done in advance. There is minimal congregational involvement.

Beemer, M., J. Davis, E. Fromm, and R. Johnston. *Responsible Faith: A Course Study for Confirmation Education and the Rite of Confirmation.* Madison, Wis.: Wisconsin Press, 1981. Available from Wisconsin Conference, United Church of Christ, 2719 Marshall Court, Madison, Wisconsin 53705.

United Church of Christ. Twenty-four one-hour sessions for senior high confirmands. Based on the Heidelberg Catechism and organized into four units of study: (a) the sacrament of baptism and the Rite of Confirmation; (b) the human condition; (c) how God deals with the human condition; and (d) the human response —gratitude.

The program is discussion-oriented, with other activities mixed in for variety. The rather detailed introduction should help prepare the leader with its basic theological background for confirmation. There is not a large amount of reading required of the student, although some research is needed for small projects. Most of the reading needs to be done by the leader. Other resources are listed in the book and are expected to be easily available to the average teacher.

Cathey, M. J., D. Koza-Woodward, G. J. Kroupa, A. Z. Hulp, et al. *The Confirmation Guidebook.* Washington, D.C.: National Capital Presbytery, 1984.

Presbyterian. This six-month program for senior high confirmands (ninth graders) can be modified to run from twelve sessions to one year. A person-oriented curriculum relates the biblical witness to the personal faith of confirmands. It combines games, discussions, elder sponsors, retreats, and various other activities in a balanced program of faith development and exploration. The curriculum is written clearly by teachers for teachers, and the lessons are well outlined and laid out. The course covers worship, the Trinity, and the Christian life of faith.

Confirmation Task Force, Department of Christian Education, Episcopal Diocese of Southern Virginia. *Confirmed to Serve: Perspectives, Approaches, Models and Resources for Confirmation Preparation.* 1986 (out of print).

Episcopalian. As the title implies, this is more a resource for those planning curricula than a fully developed program. The articles on confirmation pertain to adults, teens, and younger children. Intergenerational approaches are also considered. Overall, the contributors focus on a combination of biblical and traditional knowledge with an emphasis on experiential learning and community. Jean Rutherford summarizes in her preface: "We believe that a mature faith grows out of Christian conversion and nurturing, and that confirmation preparation is a wonderful opportunity to facilitate movement toward a deeper spiritual level." This packet had at least ten different articles, each with unique views, and it would probably be most helpful to people thinking about what type of confirmation program to set up.

Explorations into Faith: A Course for Youth Preparing to be Confirmed/Commissioned. Judith A. Sutherland, Student Workbook (A Journal). M. N. and A. S. Turnage, Leaders' Guide. Philadelphia: Geneva Press, 1977.

Presbyterian. Seventeen sessions for ninth graders. This curriculum sees confirmation as a process involving "exploring, wondering, choosing," and "doing." The pastor is the primary teacher, although "other professionally trained staff members and/or lay persons who are experienced teachers and sensitive leaders of youth also serve as teacher." Adults are seen as resource people and sponsors. There can be family involvement, and at least two retreats are recommended. The emphasis is on content.

"In offering a confirmation/commissioning class the church provides an opportunity for the young person to explore the basic meanings of the Christian faith and to be commissioned to live out that faith in the world" (Leaders' Guide, 10). The curriculum has three parts: (a) life of the congregation (3 sessions), (b) Christian heritage (10 sessions); and (c) student's personal response and decision making (4 sessions).

Huyser-Honig, Joan and Steve, *The Church Serves: Working in God's World,* and W. R. Lenters, *The Church Cares: Belonging to God's Family.* Grand Rapids, Mich.: Bible Way, CRC Publications, 1987.

Reformed. Each book contains twelve lessons for seventh- and eighth-grade confirmands, designed for forty-five- to sixty-minute sessions which can be expanded.

This set of two books offers an alternative curriculum for churches which are religiously conservative and want to stress the church's role and activity in the world. The credal/catechetical statement, "Our World Belongs to God: A Contemporary Testimony," is used extensively throughout the books, and the Reformed theology is clearly set out. The first book, *The Church Serves*, shows the students that they are valuable members of the church community and that their community plays a larger role in the society surrounding it. *The Church Cares* is oriented more toward the life of students within the church. It stresses the universality of the church, the "benefits of responsibilities" of church membership, and the need to "publicly profess" one's faith.

Each lesson is clearly outlined with purpose, perspective, and procedure statements. The program requires a minimum of supplies, and there is a straightforward format that highlights the activity/discussion and its goal. Students need to prepare ahead of time for the lessons.

The Living Catechism. 4 vols. Philadelphia: Parish Life Press, 1987.

Lutheran. Forty chapters, one chapter per session; Bible readings encouraged during the week. For confirmands in seventh through ninth grades. Organized in four volumes: (1) *Apostles' Creed;* (2) *Ten Commandments;* (3) *Lord's Prayer, Luther's Morning and Evening Prayers;* (4) *Baptism, Eucharist, Confession, Office of the Keys.*

The student books primarily offer readings, while the detailed *Leader's Guide* offers exercises for the group. The curriculum is content-oriented, and a significant amount of memorization is required of the student. Quotes from the catechisms are used extensively throughout the books. Some of the activities include roleplaying and reflection/discussion sessions. Discussion is favored over other types of activities, and the curriculum studies theology in more depth than most others.

McClelland, W. Robert. . . . *And On This Rock.* St. Louis, Mo.: Hope Church Publications, 1982.

Presbyterian. Twenty-five-week program in varied formats for confirmands in ninth grade and older. The program "seeks, through its educational, psychological, and theological assumptions, to be consistent with the best claims of the faith. Its procedures are exercises in faith in search of understanding and in search of expression through action" (David Ng, from the "Introduction"). McClelland sets forth these assumptions:

—*Confirmation needs to supplant, not replace, Sunday school.*

—*Confirmation is preparation for membership in the church.*

—*This curriculum uses the "educational philosophy of developmental psychology."*

—*It is assumed that the Christian faith is not primarily interested in nor concerned with facts about the Bible, names, places, dates, or authorship of its various books. Rather, it is concerned with an experience of "New Humanity" which the Bible speaks of as "being born again," "raised again from the death of life," and "set free."*

Since teaching must honor the uniqueness of its subject matter, and since the uniqueness of the subject matter of the Christian religion is the living experience of the New Humanity, [this program] abandons the traditional approach to Confirmation education with its emphasis on denominational history and beliefs, and seeks to make available to the student the experience of New Humanity. (vii-viii)

The curriculum is largely experiential, with the lessons split between a conceptual part, "Food for Thought," and an experiential one, "Let's Do." McClelland sets up three basic ground rules: "Trust your experience"; "share your experience with the class"; and "don't fake it." Topics covered include the church (as building, organization, faith community), faith, people, sin, Christian interpretation of history, Christology, and prayer. The author primarily sees the instructor as a resource/facilitator/model for the confirmands.

Meacham, Katharine. *Confirming Our Faith: A Confirmation Resource for the U.C.C.* New York: United Church Press, 1980. [This review is by Brenda Kinder.]

United Church of Christ. Thirty-nine chapters describing a one-year course of ninety-minute sessions for thirteen-year-old confirmands.

Developed from an extensive study of more than one thousand U.C.C. congregations, this program is a good curriculum for the teacher who runs the typical instructional-type, model classroom. It very much seems to follow the "banking" approach to learning: there is an incredible amount of information to be imparted, and the *Teacher's Guide* gives a step-by-step process of how to do this. There are plenty of suggestions for the teacher as to how planning might be done (leader does 75 percent, youth do 25 percent, with parents and other adults also involved), with an emphasis on learner-centered activities as opposed to teacher-centered activities. The material emphasizes biblical and theological themes. Students will wrestle with major theological questions, explore the Bible and learn interpretative skills, encounter some difficult doctrines, learn to question their own interpretations and responses, and find a clearer understanding of the church and how they want to relate to it at this time in their lives. There is an extensive resource section and glossary.

Neinast, Helen R., and Sidney D. Fowler. *Journey into Faith: A Confirmation Resource for Junior Highs*. Nashville: Graded Press, United Methodist Publishing House, 1984.

United Methodist. Thirteen sessions of one and one-half to two hours; can be expanded to twenty-six sessions over two years. For junior high confirmands.

This curriculum was written by a married co-pastor team. Included with the *Pastor's Guide* are several posters, a filmstrip, a cassette, materials for activities, and a game. The authors write that, "The pastor has primary responsibility for designing and teaching confirmation training. . . . In spite of the pastor's involvement in confirmation, this educational venture should not be just 'the pastor's class.' Confirmation can—and should—be the ministry of an entire congregation" (2–3). They offer ways to involve parents, families, and church members as sponsors and co-workers on committees. The adults can also join the confirmands on retreats, for church-sponsored dinners, and so forth.

Neinast and Fowler see confirmation as a commitment to the life of the church where the confirmands need to make a personal choice to commit themselves to the church. The curriculum includes journal-writing, writing one's own creed, outreach projects, retreats, and group-building exercises. The authors call attention to the need for follow-up after confirmation so that the newly confirmed members will not feel as though they had "graduated," so to speak. The sessions concentrate on personal growth, with minimal emphasis on content and memorization.

Nelson, F. Burton. *The Story of the People of God*. Chicago: Covenant Press, 1974. And Glen V. Wiberg, *Called to Be His People*. Chicago: Covenant Press, 1970.

Evangelical Covenant Church of America. Two-year program for junior high confirmands.

The Story of the People of God stresses knowledge of the Bible and its relation to the present world, with a short section on church history. This 435-page book has frequent and lengthy exercises.

Called to Be His People works on theology and life in the church. The exercises are shorter than those in the other volume, but students are asked to memorize brief passages.

Both volumes ask students to do several projects, including typed and footnoted papers. The sheer amount of material as well as its sophistication may pose problems for some junior high students. Two or three adult helpers are suggested. The major emphasis is upon learning the large amount of material in the curriculum. Many churches may find this curriculum too long and detailed for their needs.

Sawyer, Kierau, S.S.N.D. *Confirming Faith: A Faith Development Program for High School Students Preparing to Celebrate the Sacrament of Confirmation*. Notre Dame, Ind.: Ave Maria Press, 1982.

Roman Catholic. Twelve sessions for large groups of thirty to forty high-school students. Designed for the "non-professional volunteer catechist," this curriculum is explicitly Roman Catholic, making distinctions between Christians and "Catholic Christians," presumably in an effort to better define the Catholic church against the background of Protestantism in America. It hopes to prepare students to "live a life of faith" which is both "personal and communal" within the context of the faith community (33, 39). Confirmation:

> —*"is one of the sacraments of Christian initiation."*
> —*"is intimately connected with baptism . . . [and the] Eucharist."*
> —*"is the sacrament of the Holy Spirit."*
> —*"binds one more closely to the church."*
> —*"is the sacrament of Christian witness."* (8-10)

The classes are described in great detail in the course manual, making it fairly easy for volunteers. The format is that of a large group with a coordinator (the catechist) and one adult moderator for every five to ten kids. The content has clear ties to values clarification and moral development theory, especially that of L. Kohlberg. The "four basic catechetical elements" for the author are community, worship, service, and message. Service projects and retreats are included.

Related Materials

"Effective Christian Education: A National Study of Protestant Congregations—A Report for the United Church of Christ." Minneapolis: Search Institute, 1990.

The report studied six different denominations and their outlook on Christian education (Disciples of Christ, Evangelical Lutheran Church in America, Presbyterian Church in the USA, Southern Baptist Convention, United Church of Christ, and United Methodist Church). This report will help any person involved with Christian education to develop a better understanding of the issues facing the church today. It would be helpful for confirmation programs as well, especially in terms of tailoring material to be most effective with modern youth.

Roehlkepartain, Eugene C. "What Makes Faith Mature?" *The Christian Century* 107 (May 9, 1990): 496–99.

Roehlkepartain summarizes the Search Institute report, "Effective Christian Education," and adds helpful comments from several educators.

New Member's Covenant

Resource for Chapter 6, Covenantal Experience 2

Understanding that the Bible is a book of covenants between believers and God, this covenant reclaims that biblical idea in a modern way. God made a covenant with Noah that the earth would be sanctified and never again destroyed. God and Abraham made a covenant that the descendants of Abraham and Sarah would be a blessed people. God, Moses, and the people of Israel covenanted to obey God's laws, to be a holy nation, and in return God would richly bless them. Jesus promises us a new covenant based on grace and the forgiveness of sins. A covenant always has at least two parties involved, and God is always one of those partners.

As a newly confirmed member of [name of church], I hereby make this covenant with the members of the body of Christ, and with God, to try to the best of my ability to be involved in the full membership of the church.

I will try, with God's help, to be active in the following ways:

(please check areas of involvement)

_____ Pledge offering

_____ Attend worship regularly

_____ Assist in teaching Sunday School

_____ Participate in youth group

_____ Sing in church choir

_____ Greeter

_____ Worship usher

_____ Serve on church boards/committees

_____ Help to count offerings
_____ Help out with coffee hour
_____ Help in the church office
_____ Babysitting/child care
_____ Upkeep of church grounds/building
_____ Snow shoveling/lawn cutting for older church members
_____ Volunteer programs
_____ Representing church at outside meetings
_____ Other (please specify) _____

This covenant was signed by me on _____ (date)

_____

(New member's signature)

The Letter

by Charles M. Tanner

SCENE A small lounge—could be at a college, in a hotel, or even a coffee shop. Something of the like. A small table, some chairs, coffee mug, dry cream and sugar, napkin dispenser for a coffee bar or even a lounge, minus the dispenser. Books, portfolio, notebooks, briefcase for the lounge or room. A person (Kite) is sitting in a chair or at a table writing when a friend enters. Either gender can play either role.

BOX (Wanders in carrying a magazine, a paper, and a paperback book) What're you doing?

KITE (Without looking up) I'm writing a letter.

BOX (A little sarcasm) I thought you were working on a book.

KITE (Some sarcasm back) Then why ask?

BOX (Nosey, of course) Who're you writing to? (A good friend's needling) Didn't know you had any friends.

KITE (The same back) What about you?

BOX (Big smile) You're my good deed for the year.

KITE (They're having fun) When do you start?

BOX (Lack of wit response) Hah! (A beat) Who're you writing to?

KITE (Looks up) A bit nosey, aren't you?

BOX (Easily) Not nosey at all. Just curious.

KITE (Raised eyebrows) Didn't know there was a difference.

BOX (Fast and at ease) Of course there is. If I was nosey, I'd have come over, taken the paper and looked for myself. Since I'm not that kind, I asked.

KITE (Flat—part of the game retort) You didn't come over, etc., because you're lazy—that's all.

179

BOX (Laid back shrug) So I'm a tad lazy. I make up for it with my brilliant mind.

KITE (Sniffs derisively) I can hardly wait.

BOX (Mock serious) Jealousy is a sinful avocation.

KITE (Nods—back to the letter) I'll keep that in mind.

BOX (Patronizingly) Don't hide it, old buddy. Do something about it.

KITE (A hope) I'll be quiet if you will.

BOX (Happily) That's hardly fair. You *are* quiet and I have this urgent need to communicate.

KITE (Flat) Good luck.

BOX (Really interested) C'mon, who you writing to?

KITE (Nervous about Box knowing who it is) You don't really want to know.

BOX (Friendly but persistent) I really want to know. Tell me so I can relax and enjoy my laziness a bit.

KITE (Evading the question) What difference does it make? Go right straight to lazing—do not pass curiosity.

BOX (Big smile) I'm stuck there. Give—who?

KITE (Sighs) You won't believe it.

BOX (Raised eyebrows) I won't believe who you're writing to? What's not to believe? Now, I got to know. Talk. I'll pester you until I do know, you know.

KITE (Sighs again) You really won't believe it.

BOX (Quickly) I'll believe it. I'll believe it. Who?

KITE God.

BOX (Startled) I don't believe it.

KITE (Nods) I said you wouldn't.

BOX (Really struck) C'mon, you flipped your lid or something? Writing God? That's nuts.

KITE (Evenly) I don't think so.

BOX (Frowns) Why are you doing something crazy like that?

KITE (A direct look) I want to communicate with the Lord, that's why.

BOX (Up and moves about) But a letter? Don't even whisper it to someone else. They'd lock you up.

KITE (Surprised look) For wanting to communicate with God?

BOX (In fast, voice up) For writing God a letter, you goofball. A letter!

KITE (Intensely) I *have* to talk with God.

BOX (Big gesture) Then pray, for pity sake. Pray. Writing God a letter is completely loco.

KITE (Shakes head) I don't think so.

BOX (Stares at Kite) How you going to mail it? That I'd like to know. But tell me quietly. I don't want to have to break in a new roommate.

KITE (Flat) I don't intend to mail it, of course.

BOX Of course. (Stares at Kite) Then what are you going to do with it?

KITE (Shrugs) File it away I guess. It might be helpful later on.

BOX (Sniffs) In case God rifles through your file, you mean?

KITE (Thinking seriously) No, no. To see what has happened. Whether I've grown. How God has answered my prayers.

BOX (Big-eyed look) Oh. You're gonna pray too. A little insurance there, eh?

KITE (Earnestly) The letter *is* a prayer. Don't you see?

BOX (A wondering stare) Why not just pray—you know—with words? Out loud or to yourself, whatever?

KITE (Looks down, a bit sad) Because I'm not very good at it. I'm afraid my mind wanders or I get hung up on syntax, grammar, and just plain words.

BOX (The same things happen to Box of course. Answers dryly) Oh, really?

KITE (Nods honestly) Yes. I'm not very good at prayer. But I need very much to pray—well—clearly, meaningfully.

BOX (Feeling a bit chagrined) I see.

KITE (Carries on) So in order to get better at it, I've been writing letters to God. In that way it's down there on paper and even when it's not very good, not very explicit or even very clear—at least I can see what I've said. And then get an idea where I went wrong—where I missed out—in communication.

BOX   (Nods knowingly, without knowing, and waves vaguely in the face of such simple truth) I, uh, see. (Beat) How about that?

KITE   (Thoughtfully) It makes me feel close to God, somehow. I mean putting the thoughts down on paper makes them become more real in a sense. As though we were both looking at the same thing in a way I understand.

BOX   Oh. (Thinks that one out) The way you understand?

KITE   Yes. (Tries to explain) You see, when I pray in my mind or out loud, I'm often working harder at trying to say things right than I am in concentrating on saying what I really mean. You see?

BOX   (Nope) Oh sure. (Works at it though)

KITE   (Continuing) So that when I write it all out in a letter, I begin to see what it is I am saying—and in a way what I am really trying to get across.

BOX   (Noncommittally) Uh huh.

KITE   (Trying hard to be cogent) And as a result, I begin to understand me better. And to see some answers even through that understanding.

BOX   (Begins to see some light) Really.

KITE   (Working it out) As I have begun to see and understand it—at least for me—prayer is not only the citing of one's daily requests and desires, but it is an opportunity for real communication.

BOX   (Might be at that) Yeah.

KITE   (Frowns) Communication in this case doesn't mean letting God know who I am. (Laughs) Unfortunately—and maybe fortunately, too—God knows who I am. Totally. In every way.

BOX   (Hit) Ouch!

KITE   (Now warming up) Oh, yes, but we are safe in God's hands. Not to worry about that part. It is, however, terribly important that we do not kid ourselves about who we are. To be wrong is one thing. And bad enough. But to be wrong and to convince yourself that you are really right— that is awful. And highly dangerous.

BOX   (Gulps) I see your point.

KITE (Shrugs) So I write God letters. And in those letters I either see me better or find I'm leaving something out—which means I'm back trying to kid myself again. When that happens, I backtrack and find what I've left out.

BOX (Looks away) I don't think I'd like that.

KITE (Nods) I know. I don't either. (Thoughtfully) But I guess it's a case of whether you'll have the operation—or the cancer.

BOX (Gulps) You have a certain way with words.

KITE (Surprised) Really?

BOX (Smarting) Yeah, and you ought to do something about it.

KITE (Nods) I guess so. (Looks at the letter) That's why I've found it very valuable, very helpful to write letters as prayers.

BOX (Has been thinking very hard) Yeah. Oh yeah.

KITE (With a half-embarrassed grin) It is kinda crazy, I suppose.

BOX (Gets up and starts across the room to the exit, minus papers) Uh huh. Real crazy.

KITE (Frowns) Hope I didn't upset you. (Concerned) Uh, where you going?

BOX (At the door, turns and looks at friend) I'm going to get a pen and some paper if you must know. (Sighs heavily and exits. Offstage we hear) Crazy, yeah! Like a fox—or maybe a Paul!

(And then *curtain* is closed as Kite has a look that is full of wonder at what happened)

The End

For further information, please contact the publisher or Charles M. Tanner, P.O. Box 2900, Oxnard, CA 93034-2900.

Notes

Chapter 1. Confirmation as Rite of Passage

1. Christopher Nichols, at a United Church of Christ's Ohio Confirmation Workshop led by William R. Myers in April 1990.

2. The Search Institute's examination of five mainline denominations' teachings of religion suggest that "involvement in Christian education ends for most Protestants at the 9th grade." Reported by Michael Hirsley, *Chicago Tribune*, May 23, 1990, sec. 2, p. 7.

3. Ibid.

4. Aidan Kavanaugh, *Confirmation: Origins and Reform* (New York: Pueblo, 1988), 3.

5. Christine Brusselmans, "Introduction," in *A History of the Catechumenate: The First Six Centuries* by Michael Dujaner (New York: Sadlier, 1979), 6.

6. Frank W. Klos, *Confirmation and First Communion* (St. Louis: Concordia, 1968), 37–38.

7. Joseph P. Christopher, *St. Augustine: The First Catechetical Instruction* (Baltimore: J. H. Durst, 1946), 15.

8. Leonel L. Mitchell, "Christian Initiation: The Reformation Period," in *Made, Not Born: New Perspectives on Christian Initiation and the Catechumenate*, by The Murphy Center for Liturgical Research (Notre Dame, Ind.: University of Notre Dame Press, 1976), 91.

9. Richard Baxter, *Practical Works*, vol. 14 (London, 1830), as quoted in Philip Edgecumbe Hughes, *Confirmation in the Church Today* (Grand Rapids: William B. Eerdmans, 1973), 16.

10. Arthur C. Repp, *Confirmation in the Lutheran Church* (St. Louis: Concordia Press, 1964), 81.

11. Frank Klos, *Confirmation and First Communion: A Study Book* (Minneapolis: Augsburg Publishing House, 1968), 70.

12. Repp, *Confirmation in the Lutheran Church*, 78.

13. Ibid., 79–80.

14. Ibid., 81

15. Ibid., 81.

16. Sören Kierkegaard, *The Point of View,* trans. Walter Lowrie (London: Oxford University Press, 1939), 74.

17. Sören Kierkegaard, *A Kierkegaard Anthology,* ed. Robert [Walter] Bretall, trans. Walter Lowrie (Princeton, N.J.: Princeton University Press, 1946), 454.

18. The best single volume on the invention of adolescence is Joseph F. Kett, *Rites of Passage: Adolescence in America, 1790 to the Present* (New York: Basic Books, 1977).

Chapter 2. Becoming and Belonging

1. Daniel B. Stevick, "Christian Initiation: Post-Reformation to the Present Era," in *Made, Not Born,* 108.

2. Klos, *Confirmation and First Communion,* 54.

3. Laurie Waits, quoted in Tom Montgomery-Fate, *Building Worlds/ Challenging Boundaries: Appalachia Service Project, Inc.* (Johnson City, Tenn.: Appalachia Service Project, 1991), 32.

4. Quoted in Montgomery-Fate, *Building Worlds,* 7.

5. William R. Myers, foreword in Montgomery-Fate, *Building Worlds,* vi–vii.

Chapter 3. Embodying Four Core Conditions

1. In my opinion, the best peer ministry book is still Bryan Reynolds, *A Chance to Serve: A Leader's Manual for Peer Ministry* (Winona, Minn.: St. Mary's Press, 1983).

2. David R. Shaffer, *Social and Personality Development* (Monterey, Calif.: Brooks/Cole, 1979), 543.

3. *Parable* (1964), a film produced for the New York World's Fair, available from Mass Media Ministries, 2116 Charles St., Baltimore, Maryland 21218, 1-800-828-8825.

4. The best mentoring model currently available with confirmation in mind is written by William Willimon and reviewed in chapter 11 of this book.

5. This approach reflects Thomas Groome's idea of "Shared Christian Praxis." See, in particular, chapter 9 in his book *Christian Religious Education: Sharing Our Story and Vision* (San Francisco: Harper and Row, 1980).

6. Read about hospitality and education in Henri J. M. Nouwen's *Reaching Out: The Three Movements of the Spiritual Life* (New York: Doubleday, 1975).

7. On the persistent accommodation to the dominant culture by the middle-class, white congregation, read William R. Myers, *Black and White Styles of Youth Ministry: Two Congregations in America* (New York: The Pilgrim Press, 1991).

8. William R. Myers, *Theological Themes of Youth Ministry* (New York: The Pilgrim Press, 1987), 46.

Chapter 4. Pastor Jim's Strategy

1. For statistics on the small church experience, check Carl S. Dudley, *Making the Small Church Effective* (Nashville: Abingdon Press, 1978).

2. See, for small churches, Robert B. Coote, ed., *Mustard-Seed Churches: Making the Small Church Effective* (Minneapolis: Fortress Press, 1990).

Chapter 6. Youth, Spirituality, and the Church

1. Philip Phenix, "Transcendence and the Curriculum," in *Conflicting Conceptions of Curriculum*, ed. E. W. Eisner and E. Vallance (Berkeley: McCutchan, 1974).

2. John Dewey, *A Common Faith* (New Haven: Yale University Press, 1934).

3. L. S. Vygotsky, *Mind in Society: The Development of Higher Psychological Processes*, trans. Michael Cole, Vera John-Steiner, Sylvia Scribner, and Ellen Souberman (Cambridge: Harvard University Press, 1978).

4. See William R. Myers, "Youth between Culture and Church," *Theology Today* 47, no. 4 (January 1991): 400–409; and "The Church in the World: Models of Youth Ministry," *Theology Today* 44, no. 1 (April 1987): 103–11.

Chapter 7. We Covenant with the Lord and One with Another

1. See John Bradner, *Symbols of Church Seasons and Days* (Wilton, Conn.: Morehouse-Barlow Company, 1977) or Dean Moe, *Christian Symbols Handbook: Commentary and Patterns for Traditional and Contemporary Symbols* (Minneapolis: Augsburg, 1985).

2. "Hands, Imposition of," in *The Oxford Dictionary of the Christian Church*, ed. F. L. Cross (London: Oxford University Press, 1957), 607.

3. Sidney Simon, *I Am Lovable and Capable: A Modern Allegory on the Classical Putdown* (Niles, Ill.: Argus Communications, 1973).

Chapter 8. Experiencing the Tradition

1. *Ecce Homo* (1962) Paulist Productions, P.O. Box 1057, Pacific Palisades, Calif. 90272.

2. Information on history of Council of Chalcedon can be found in R. V. Sellers, *The Council of Chalcedon: A Historical and Doctrinal Survey* (London: SPCK, 1961).

3. *Where Luther Walked* (1982), Mass Media Ministries, 2116 Charles St., Baltimore, Maryland 21218, 1-800-828-8825.

4. "Ten from the Top," in William R. Myers, *Strategies for Youth Programs, Senior High*, vol. 1, ed. Judy R. Fletcher (Philadelphia: Geneva Press, 1978), 166–74.

Chapter 9. Pilgrimage

1. *The Book of Common Prayer* (New York: Henry Holt & Co., 1992), 300.

2. *Strategies for Senior Highs*, vol. 1, ed. Judy R. Fletcher (Philadelphia: Geneva Press, 1978), 143–45; originally designed by William R. Myers at Flossmoor Community Church, Evanston, Illinois.

3. Mark Link, *Prayer Paths: Search for Serenity and God in an Age of Stress* (Allen, Tex.: Tabor Pub., 1990), and Mark Link, *Vision Two Thousand: Praying Scripture in a Contemporary Way* (Allen, Tex.: Tabor Pub., 1992).

4. *Godspell* vocal scores are available from H. Leonard Publishing Co., 7777 W. Bluemound Road, P.O. Box 13819, Milwaukee, WI 53213, 1-800-221-2774. Permission for performance is available from Theatre Maximus, 212-765-5913.

Chapter 10. Ministry

1. Merton Strommen, *Five Cries of Youth* (San Francisco: Harper and Row, 1988). See also Strommen's *Five Cries of Parents* (San Francisco: Harper and Row, 1985).

2. H. Moltmann, *The Church in the Power of the Spirit* (New York: Harper and Row, 1977), 301.

3. This experience was initially designed by Myers, *Strategies for Youth Programs*, 175–77.

4. CROP, c/o Church World Service, P.O. Box 968, Elkhart, Ind. 46515.

Selected Bibliography

Bonhoeffer, Dietrich. *Letters and Papers from Prison*. Ed. Eberhard Bethge. New York: Macmillan, 1953.

Brueggemann, Walter. *The Bible Makes Sense*. Winona, Minn.: St. Mary's Press, 1977.

Carroll, Jackson W. *Small Churches Are Beautiful*. San Francisco: Harper and Row, 1977.

Christopher, Joseph P. *St. Augustine: The First Catechetical Instruction*. Baltimore: J. H. Durst, 1946.

Coote, Robert B., ed. *Mustard-Seed Churches: Making the Small Church Effective*. Minneapolis: Fortress Press, 1990.

Dewey, John. *A Common Faith*. New Haven: Yale University Press, 1934.

Dudley, Carl S. *Making the Small Church Effective*. Nashville: Abingdon Press, 1978.

Dujarier, Michael. *A History of the Catechumenate: The First Six Centuries*. New York: Sadlier, 1979.

Eisner, E. W., and E. Vallance. *Conflicting Conceptions of Curriculum*. Berkeley: McCutchan, 1974.

Foltz, Nancy T., ed. *Religious Education in the Small Membership Church*. Birmingham: Religious Education Press, 1990.

Foster, Richard J. *Celebration of Discipline: The Path to Spiritual Growth*. San Francisco: Harper San Francisco, 1988.

Groome, Thomas. *Christian Religious Education: Sharing Our Story and Vision*. San Francisco: Harper and Row, 1980.

Hauerwas, Stanley, and William H. Willimon. *Resident Aliens*. Nashville: Abingdon Press, 1989.

Holderness, Ginny Ward. *Youth Ministry: The New Team Approach*. Atlanta: John Knox Press, 1981.

Hughes, Philip Edgecumbe. *Confirmation in the Church Today*. Grand Rapids: William B. Eerdmans, 1973.

Johnson, Suzanne. "Education in the Image of God." In *Theological Approaches to Christian Education*, edited by Jack L. Seymour and Donald E. Miller. Nashville: Abingdon Press, 1990.

Kavanaugh, Aidan. *Confirmation: Origins and Reform*. New York: Pueblo, 1988.

Kett, Joseph F. *Rites of Passage: Adolescence in America, 1790 to the Present.* New York: Basic Books, 1977.

Klos, Frank. *Confirmation and First Communion: A Study Book.* Minneapolis: Augsburg Publishing House, 1968.

Link, Mark. *Prayer Paths: Search for Serenity and God in an Age of Stress.* Allen, Tex.: Tabor Pub., 1990.

————. *Vision Two Thousand: Praying Scripture in a Contemporary Way.* Allen, Tex.: Tabor Pub., 1992.

Moltmann, H. *The Church in the Power of the Spirit.* New York: Harper and Row, 1975.

Montgomery-Fate, Tom. *Building Worlds/Challenging Boundaries: Appalachia Service Project, Inc.* Johnson City, Tenn.: Appalachia Service Project, 1991.

Moore, Joseph, and James Emswiler. *Handbook for Peer Ministry.* New York: Paulist Press, 1982.

Murphy Center for Liturgical Research. *Made, Not Born: New Perspectives on Christian Initiation and the Catechumenate.* Notre Dame, Ind.: University of Notre Dame Press, 1976.

Myers, William R. *Black and White Styles of Youth Ministry: Two Congregations in America.* New York: The Pilgrim Press, 1991.

————. "The Church in the World: Models of Youth Ministry." *Theology Today* 44, no. 1 (April 1987): 103–11.

————. "Ten from the Top." In *Strategies for Youth Programs, Senior High.* Vol. 1. Edited by Judy R. Fletcher. Philadelphia: Geneva Press, 1978.

————. *Theological Themes of Youth Ministry.* New York: The Pilgrim Press, 1987.

————. "Youth between Culture and Church." *Theology Today* 47, no. 4 (January 1991): 400–409.

Nouwen, Henri J. M. *Reaching Out: The Three Movements of the Spiritual Life.* New York: Doubleday, 1975.

The Oxford Dictionary of the Christian Church. Edited by F. L. Cross. London: Oxford University Press, 1957.

Repp, Arthur C. *Confirmation in the Lutheran Church.* St Louis: Concordia Press, 1964.

Reynolds, Bryan. *A Chance to Serve: A Leader's Manual for Peer Ministry.* Winona, Minn.: St. Mary's Press, 1983.

Sawicki, Marianne. "Tradition and Sacramental Education." In *Theological Approaches to Christian Education*, edited by Jack L. Seymour and Donald E. Miller. Nashville: Abingdon Press, 1990.

Schaller, Lyle. *The Small Church Is Different.* Nashville: Abingdon Press, 1982.

Seymour, Jack L., and Donald E. Miller. *Theological Approaches to Christian Education.* Nashville: Abingdon Press, 1990.

Shaffer, David R. *Social and Personality Development.* Monterey, Calif.: Brooks/Cole, 1979.

Simon, Sidney. *I Am Lovable and Capable: A Modern Allegory on the Classical Putdown.* Niles, Ill.: Argus Communications, 1973.

Soelle, Dorothee. *Death by Bread Alone: Texts and Reflections on Religious Experiences.* Philadelphia: Fortress Press, 1975.

Strommen, Merton. *Five Cries of Parents.* San Francisco: Harper and Row, 1985.

―――― . *Five Cries of Youth.* San Francisco: Harper and Row, 1988.

Tanner, Charles. "The Letter" (play). P.O. Box 2900, Oxnard, CA 93034-2900.

Vygotsky, L. S. *Mind in Society: The Development of Higher Psychological Processes.* Trans. Michael Cole et al. Cambridge: Harvard University Press, 1978.

Wagner, Johannes, ed. *Adult Baptism and the Catechumenate.* New York: Paulist Press, 1967.

Whitehead, James D., and Evelyn Eaton Whitehead. *Method in Ministry: Theological Reflection and Christian Ministry.* San Francisco: Harper and Row, 1980.

Wilde, James, ed. *Confirmed as Children, Affirmed as Teens: The Order of Initiation.* Chicago: Liturgy Training Publications, 1990.

Willimon, William H., and Robert L. Welson. *Preaching and Worship in the Small Church.* Nashville: Abingdon Press, 1980.

Index

Acts 6:1–6, 8:15–17, 8:19, 78
Adolescence: becoming in, 11–21, 56; belonging in, 11–21, 141; confirmation as rite of passage for, 3–9; cultural invention of, 55–56; self–esteem in, 141; in Western society, 12–13. *See also* Youth
Ads, 144
Adulthood, confirmation as rite of passage into, 3–9
Advent, traditions surrounding, 72–73
Affirm, 168
Alexandria Catechetical School, 5
Amos 2:6, 122
Amos 5:21–25, 153
And on This Rock (McClelland), 171–72
Augustine, St., 5, 116

Baptism, 91; covenantal significance of, 13; and laying on of hands, 78; and Puritanism, 14; role of church in, 54; separation from confirmation, 5–6; symbolism of, 117–20
Baxter, Richard, 6
Beatitudes, 87
Becoming, 11–21, 52, 56
Beemer, M., 168–69
Belonging, 11–21, 52, 141
Bible Makes Sense (Brueggemann), 61

Bishop of Hippo, 5
Body sculpture, 121–24, 125–26
Bondage, experiencing, 148–50
Bonhoeffer, Dietrich, 91
Brainstorming, 98–99
Brueggemann, Walter, 61
Building Worlds/Challenging Boundaries (Montgomery-Fate), 17–18

Called to Be His People (Wilberg), 174
Calvin, John, 6–8
"Catechetical Instruction: Using Media in Catechism" (Lindberg and Havice), 162
Cathey, M. J., 169
Celebration of Discipline: The Path to Spiritual Growth (Foster), 128
Chain letter, as analogy for explaining laying on of hands, 77–79
Chalcedon, Council of, 95–97
Children's ward, 154–55
Christmas, traditions surrounding, 72–73
Church: confirmation as rite of passage into, 3–9; early, 4–5; merger of state and, 5–6; structure of confirmation in small, 24, 35–43
Church Cares: Belonging to God's Family, The (Lenters), 170–71

Church leadership, involvement of youth in, 65

Church Serves: Working in God's World, The (Huyser-Honig), 170–71

Church World Service, 150

Community involvement, 30–31, 32–33. *See also* Ministry

Complete Works of Robert Frost, 127

Confirmation: in American context, 8–9; as compulsory, 3; and congregational identity, 12–14; core conditions for, 14–21; in early church, 4–5; expectations of, 3; formats of, 23; leaders in, 36; models of, 37–40, 41–42, 45–47; parents on, 49; recollections of, 3–4; in Reformation, 6–8; as rite of passage, 3–9; separation from baptism, 5–6; service for, 7–8, 16; in state churches, 6; structure of, in small church, 36–37; team approach to, 14, 23–33; three-phase, multi-year experience in, 40–41. *See also* Curriculum

Confirmation and First Communion: A Study Book (Klos), 161–62

Confirmation Guidebook (Cathey et al.), 169

Confirmation Ministry—A Family Life-Style: A Handbook of Resources and Ideas (Myers), 163

Confirmation Today: Ten Affirmations (Wingeier), 166

Confirmed as Children, Affirmed as Teens (Wilde), 3

Confirmed to Serve: Perspectives, Approaches, Models, and Resources for Confirmation Preparation, 169–70

Confirming Faith: A Faith Development Program for High School Students Preparing to

Celebrate the Sacrament of Confirmation (Sawyer), 174–75

Confirming Our Faith: A Confirmation Resource (Meacham), 172–73

Congregational identity, 12–14

Constantine, conversion of, 5

Contract, and differences between covenant, 69–70

Core conditions. *See* Covenant; Ministry; Pilgrimage; Tradition

1 Corinthians 12:21–31, 135

Covenant, 14, 19, 20, 31–32, 46, 53, 69–70; differences between contract and, 69–70; "Hanging of the Greens," 72–73; Heirs of the Covenant experience, 71–72; history interviews, 73–75; retreat as focus event on, 79–90; sanctuary scavenger hunt, 75–77; world's greatest chain letter, 77–79

Covenanting, 64

"Crankie," 81

CROP walk, 150–52

Cross-generational leadership, 51–52

Cultures, dueling, 47–51

Curriculum, 3, 61–62; Episcopalian, 170; Evangelical Covenant Church of America, 174; Lutheran, 161–62, 163, 168, 171; Presbyterian, 4, 164–65, 167–68, 169, 170, 172; Reformed, 171; Roman Catholic, 159, 162, 174–75; United Church of Christ, 160–61, 163–64, 169, 173; United Methodist, 165–66, 173–74

Daily life, making connection between faith and, 71–72

Davis, J., 168–69

Death by Bread Alone (Soelle), 23

Debriefing, 84
Deuteronomy 34:9, 69
Dewey, John, 62
Diakonia, 28, 142
Dunning, James B., 159

Ecce Homo, 93, 94
Ephesians 4:1–6, 135
Episcopalian curriculum, 170
Evangelical Covenant Church of
  America curriculum, 174
Exodus 3:5, 122
Exodus 32:1–6, 145
Exodus 32:1–6, 7–8, 15–26, 146
*Explorations into Faith: A Course for
  Youth Preparing to Be Confirmed/
  Commissioned* (Sutherland and
  Turnage), 170

Faith, making connection
  between daily life and, 71–72
Five Cries of Youth (Strommen),
  141
Food, 89
Footwashing, 155–58
Foster, Richard J., 128
Fowler, Sidney D., 173–74
Fromm, E., 168–69

Galatians 3:10–12, 153
Gandhi, 95
Genesis 4, 31
Genesis 6:11–14, 7:1–5, 11–12,
  17–24, 126
Genesis 8:6–12, 20–22, 127
Godspell, 138
Golden calves, making, 143–46
Good Samaritan, parable of, 29,
  30, 32, 92
Gorrell, Brenda, 160–61

"Hanging of the Greens," 72–73
Hauerwas, Stanley, 11, 167
Havice, M. J., 162

Hebrews 1:1, 96
Hebrews 5:7, 96
Heirs of the Covenant experience,
  71–72
History interviews, 73–75
Holderness, Ginny Ward, 45
Holy Spirit, 57–59, 77–79
Hospitality, 32
Hospital visits, 154–55
Hulp, A. Z., 169
Huyser-Honig, Joan and Steve,
  170–71

I Am Lovable and Capable (Simon),
  83
Icebreakers, 98
Immersion, 5
*Initiation to Adulthood: An Ancient
  Rite of Passage in Contemporary
  Form* (Roberts), 163–64

Jesus: answering question of who
  is, 93–95; and the Council of
  Chalcedon, 95–97; use of
  parables by, 28–31, 82, 97–100
John 3:17–19, 32–35, 38–41, and
  43–44, 81
John 3:31, 36–38, 95
John 11:1, 81
John 13:1–17, 155
John 19:26–27, 28–30, 96
Johnson, R., 168–69
Johnson, Suzanne, 115
Journal writing, 28
*Journey into Faith: A Confirmation
  Resource for Junior Highs*
  (Neinast and Fowler), 173–74
Journeys of Faith, 166–67

Kerygma, 28, 142
Kierkegaard, Sören, 8
King, Martin Luther, 95
Klos, Frank W., 161–62
Knox, John, 6

Koinonia, 28, 142
Koza-Woodward, D., 169
Kroupa, G. J., 169

Laying on of hands, 77–79
Layperson, involvement of, 14,
31–32, 38, 42, 85
Leadership: cross-generational,
51–52; involvement of youth in
church, 65; Lone Ranger style
of, 36
Lenders, W. R., 170–71
"Letter, The" (Tanner), 131–34,
179–83
Letters and Papers from Prison
(Bonhoeffer), 91
Life-texts, 124
Lindberg, A. R., 162
Link, Mark, 128
Living Catechism, 171
"Lone Ranger" style of leader-
ship, 36
Lord's Prayer, 131–34
Luke 3, 118
Luke 6:27–31, 95
Luke 10, 29, 31, 153
Luke 11:1–4, 132
Luke 15:22–24, 122
Luke 17:20–21, 95
Luke 20:26–29, 96
Luke 22:24–27, 153
Luther, Martin, 15–16, 101; and
the Reformation, 101–2
Lutheran curriculum, 161–62, 163,
168, 171

McClelland, W. Robert, 171–72
Making Disciples (Willimon),
166–67
Mark 1, 118
Mark 1:14–20, 135
Mark 3:1–6, 7–12, 4:39, 95
Mark 8, 93, 95
Mark 10:16, 78

Matthew 2:13–17, 153
Matthew 5, 87, 95
Matthew 6:5–15, 132
Matthew 24:1–14, 95
Matthew 25:31–46, 153
Matthew 27, 96
Matthew 28:19, 118
Maze activity, 136–37
Meacham, Katharine, 172–73
Meals, 85, 89
Meditative prayer, 127–31
Mentoring, 14, 31–32, 38, 50–51,
53–54, 55, 85
Metanoia, 4, 5
Method in Ministry (Whitehead
and Whitehead), 35
Ministry, 17–18, 19, 21, 32–33,
141–58; children's ward visits,
154–55; CROP walk in, 150–52;
in early church, 142–43; foot-
washing as focus event on,
155–58; "Let My People Go,"
146–50; making golden calves,
143–46; service projects in,
152–54
Moltmann, H., 143
Montgomery-Fate, Tom, 17–18
Murphy Center for Liturgical
Research, 162
Music, 100–101
Myers, Victor A., 163

National Council of Churches,
150
Neinast, Helen R., 173–74
Nelson, F. Burton, 174
"New Member's Covenant," 64,
177–78
New Wine, New Wineskins:
Exploring the RCIA: Pastoral
Implications of the Rite of
Christian Initiation of Adults
(Dunning), 159
Ng, David, 167

Outdoor hikes, 83, 146–50
Overnight "lock-in," 134–39

"Paper Bag-not-ready-for-prime-
time" theater, 82
Parable, 28, 30, 31
Parables, 28–31, 82, 97–100
Parents: church participation of,
47–50, 52; on confirmation, 49
Partner exercises, 85–86
Peer ministry model, 42
Penny-posters, 15
Personal covenants, 27
Phenix, Philip, 61–62
Pietism, 16–17
Pilgrimage, 16–17, 19, 20–21, 32,
48, 49, 57–59, 115–39; and
baptism, 117–20; and flooded
moments, 124–27; and holy
ground, 120–24; and "The
Letter," 131–34, 179–83; and
meditative prayer, 127–31;
overnight lock-in as focus event
on, 134–39
Politics, 59–60; of worship, 52–54
Prayer, meditative, 127–31
Presbyterian curriculum, 4,
164–65, 166, 167–68, 169, 170,
172
Proximal development, zone of,
62
Puritan movement, 14

Rational learning, 115
Reflection, 85
Reformation, 101–2; confirmation
setting in, 6–8
Reformed curriculum, 171
Resident Aliens (Hauerwas and
Willimon), 11
*Resident Aliens: Life in the Christian
Colony* (Hauerwas), 167
*Responsible Faith: A Course Study
for Confirmation Education and*

the Rite of Confirmation (Beemer,
Davis, Fromm, and Johnson),
168–69
Retreat, 65, 79–90; experience
process, 80–90; preparation/
lead time, 80; setting for, 80
Roberts, William O., 163–64
Roman Catholic curriculum, 159,
162, 174–75
Romans 12:1–8, 135
Royko, Mike, 95

Sacrament, concept of, 118
Salem Church Covenant (1629),
70
"Sardines," 137–38
Sawicki, Marianne, 141
Sawyer, Kierau, 174–75
Scaffolding, 62–63
Scavenger hunt, sanctuary, 75–77
Service, involvement of youth in,
65–66. *See also* Ministry
Service projects, 152–54
Simon, Sidney, 81, 83
Simulation games, 83–85, 97
*Six Designs for Local Church
Confirmation Programs* (Gorrell),
160–61
Skits, 99
Small Catechism, 15–16
Smith, Kent L., 164
Soelle, Dorothee, 23
Spener, Philip, 16
"Squirms," 87–88
State, merger of, and church,
5–6
Story of the People of God, The
(Nelson), 174
Strommen, Merton, 141
Sutherland, Judith A., 170
Symbolism: and Advent/
Christmas, 72–73; of baptism,
117–20; and scavenger hunt,
75–77

Tanner, Charles M., 179–83
Team concept, 14, 23–33, 45–60
Ten Commandments, 102–13
Thompson, George B., Jr., 165
Three-phase, multi-year confirmation experience, 40–41; critical reflection on, 41–42
Tradition, 15–16, 19, 20, 32, 46, 47, 54–57, 91–113; Council of Chalcedon on, 95–97; encountering parables, 97–100; singing the Lord's song in, 100–101; Ten Commandments as focus event on, 102–13; who is Jesus activities, 93–95
Tradition and Sacramental Education (Sawicki), 141
Transcendence, 61–62
Transformational experiences, 55
"Trust walk," 146–50
Turnage, A. S., 170
Turnage, M. N., 170

United Church of Christ curriculum, 160–61, 163–64, 169, 173
United Methodist curriculum, 165–66, 173–74

Videotaping history interviews, 73–75
Vocatio, 17

Vygotsky, L. S., 62

Watson, Lila, 18
"Welcome the confirmands" party, 65
Where Luther Walked, 101–2
Whitehead, Evelyn Eaton, 35
Whitehead, James, 35
Wiberg, Glen V., 174
Wilde, James, 3
Willimon, William H., 11, 165–66, 167
Wingeier, Douglas E., 166
Worship: involvement of youth in, 66, 88; politics of, 52–54

You: Prayer for Beginners and Others Who Have Forgotten How (Link), 128
Youth: involvement of, in church, 49–51, 52–54, 59–60, 63; involvement of, in church leadership, 65; involvement of, in existing youth groups, 64–65; involvement of, in service, 65–66; involvement of, in worship, 66; vocational gifts of, 64. *See also* Adolescence
Youth groups, including youth in existing, 64–65
Youth Ministry: The New Team Approach (Holderness), 45